Christmas 2009

To Finn,
For a little laugh at our crazy country.
Have a wonderful Christmas with all your great girls.
Love Pam + Arthur.

The best of hayibo.com

Hayibo!

Breaking news. Into lots of little pieces.

The best of hayibo.com

Hayibo!

Breaking news. Into lots of little pieces.

First published by Jacana Media (Pty) Ltd in 2009

10 Orange Street
Sunnyside
Auckland Park 2092
South Africa
+2711 628 3200
www.jacana.co.za

© Hayibo.com, 2009

All rights reserved.

ISBN 978-1-77009-689-9

Design by Laugh it Off (www.laughitoff.co.za)
Printed by ABC Press, Epping, Cape Town
Job no. 000959

See a complete list of Jacana titles at www.jacana.co.za

The Office of Former President Thabo Mbeki

Room 101, Corridor 9, Somewhere dark, Pretoria, Ph: 0800-DENY

Foreword

Dear Hayibo.com

Please excuse the typeface but Jacob has confiscated my laptop. The Pahads brought me this typewriter hidden in a cake but some of the letters got strawberry jam on them and they ~~stritrie~~ stick. Thank you for asking me to write the foreword to your collection of satirical news articles. I also enjoy humour. Here is a joke:

Where did Joe Modise keep his armies? Up his sleevies.

Having said that I must stress that I do not know, and have never known, anything about anything involving armies or the purchasing of weapons of any sort. It was all ███████ ██████s idea, but he will be reading this before it gets posted so he will probably censor out that bit. He is such a twat.

For now though I am quite content here in the basement of ████████ █████. They are treating me well, and I have taken to writing Haikus to pass the time until I am King again. Would you like to see one?

>Zuma shafted me
>Nobody understood me
>Why are they so thick?

Here is another one. This one is less political as I am trying to be less bitter:

>Spring rain on meadows
>New life is beginning here
>Traitors will all pay.

Best wishes and good luck with the book,

Mr T. Mbeki, Esq.

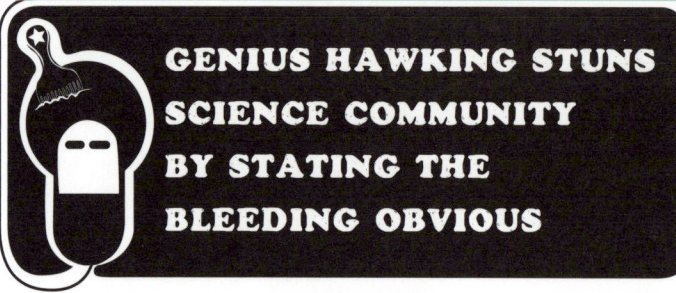

GENIUS HAWKING STUNS SCIENCE COMMUNITY BY STATING THE BLEEDING OBVIOUS

JOHANNESBURG. Acclaimed physicist Stephen Hawking stunned the scientific community last night when he publicly stated the bleeding obvious. Hawking, who is in South Africa to adjudicate a beach volleyball tournament, told appalled media that Nelson Mandela's role in ushering in democracy was "one of the greatest achievements of the twentieth century".

Hawking, who speaks with the aid of a computer, was quoted in South Africa's 'Sunday Times' as telling Mandela that he admired how the former president had "managed to find a peaceful solution to a situation that seemed doomed to disaster."

It was then that he slipped in the "greatest achievements" shocker.

However, stunned and embarrassed journalists had little time to squirm, as Hawking continued with, "If only the Israelis and the Palestinians could do the same."

According to Professor Heinrich Lindt of the European Union's elite Committee for Astrophysics and Hard Sums, it was the first time that Prof. Hawking has stated the bleeding obvious.

"I don't know what to say," a visibly distressed Prof. Lindt told media this morning in Strasbourg. "His colleagues and I are deeply traumatised.

"We train for years to avoid stating the bleeding obvious, and to see it all frittered away like that...It's awful."

He said he hoped Hawking's use of "broadsheet sentiments and the most over-indulged platitudes ever dredged up by mediocre opinion hawkers" was a once-off anomaly, and not a sign of some deterioration in a mind that is widely acknowledged to be one of the greatest of all time.

Meanwhile fellow physicist Dr Fritz Blatz of the Steve Gutenberg Centre for Particle Particulars said that Hawking had wasted an opportunity to postulate new theories on the workings of the universe.

"When he said 'If only the Israelis and the Palestinians could...' I was on the edge of my seat," said Dr Blatz.

"It's a fantastic jumping-off point for so much speculation. If only the Israelis and the Palestinians could...be used as fuel for a gigantic interstellar space portal! If only the Israelis and the Palestinians could...be shrunk to one one-hundredth of their size, and sold as children's pets, like ants, and you could watch them fight it out in a little diorama, sort of like an ant-farm but with tiny little model tanks and guard towers, and you'd only have to feed and water them once a month.

"That's what I call worthwhile speculation. But what does he give us? 'If only the Israelis and the Palestinians could do the same'. It's so banal. And it's not even ironic-banal, like that whole science dork understatement thing. It's just depressing."

Meanwhile a spokesman for Prof. Hawking would neither confirm nor deny a report that the scientist had approached Mr Mandela for lessons on how to state the bleeding obvious in such as way as to make it sound profound. ✪

search results related to: hawking volleyball

BAFANA BAFANA UP PROGRESS TARGET FROM ABJECT, HOPE TO BE AWFUL BY 2010

ACCRA. As the 26th African Cup of Nations tournament gets under way in Ghana, a fired-up South African football team has committed itself to new progress goals, upping its targets from 2007's 'Abject' to a more aggressive 'Pitiful' in 2008.

However, the South African Football Association were quick to add that the national team would not rest on their laurels should they become Pitiful in 2008.

www.hayibo.com

"Bafana Bafana is on an upward curve, like a banana," said Ace Mashabane, deputy assistant coach. "We have clear targets. For instance, by 2009 we want to be Dismal, and by 2010, we sincerely hope to be Awful." Bafana Bafana are currently ranked twelve places lower than Uzbekistan, a country in which football is taboo and all grass pitches are reserved for the exclusive use of the presidential camel. However, Mashabane says that the South African Football Association remains positive about the future of local soccer.

"The thing going for us is that we have got ishibobo skills," said Mashabane "Our guys can bounce a ball on their knee for hours. I've seen it done."

Asked why Bafana Bafana had failed to win a major tournament for over a decade, Mashabane said that "poisonous external ideologies" needed to be kept out of the local game.

"This thing of kicking the ball into the net, this is a Eurocentric tradition," he said. "The South Americans also have picked this up. It is very sad. But so far we have managed to resist this, and embrace our own African traditions."

He said these generally involved highly complex stationary dribbling skills, and kicking the ball over the net.

"It is football ubuntu," added Mashabane. "Ubuntu literally means 'I have missed the penalty, because you have missed the penalty, because if we all miss the penalty then no-one can be accountable.'" ✪

search results related to: bafana banana

DEAD RIGHT-WINGER NAMED AS HNP CANDIDATE AS HE REFLECTS STATE OF PARTY

PRETORIA. The right-wing Herstigte Nasionale Party has named deceased former leader Jaap Marais as its presidential candidate in this month's election, saying that he embodies the state of the party. The HNP was founded in 1969 in protest against the Apartheid government's "pansy-assed liberal" policy of using only semi-automatic weapons on black civilians.

The announcement was made this morning as the HNP's four active members celebrated the party's 40th anniversary at its headquarters in the stands of the Middelburg Municipal Dog Track.

Marais, who regularly referred to B.J. Vorster as "that Jew-loving homo", died in 2000 when an ox-wagon he was tuning slipped off its jack and crushed him.

His death was a body blow to the party that had once denounced P.W. Botha as a "Communist fornicator hell-bent on forcing Satan's teat – television – into the pink mouths of our white babies". A bitter power struggle ensued, during which the remaining six members sent each other curdled milk-tarts and bottles of fig jam with lids too tight to open.

However, the deaths of two more members – both from strokes after accidental exposure to SABC1 – has reportedly unified the party.

Speaking to journalists this morning, HNP spokesman Wolraad Strond said that there had been only one suitable candidate to contest the coming election. "We had a long look at the party, and we brainstormed some words to describe it," he said. "It was mostly stuff like 'under ground', 'dead', 'buried', that kind of thing. "And obviously Jaap represents all of that really well.

"Plus he's really patient," said Strond. "If he loses this time round he's happy to wait until 2014. He's not going anywhere."

However, Strond conceded that the party might miss the election altogether as it was struggling to raise the R500,000 deposit required by the Independent Electoral Commission. "We've got R86 so far," he said, thanking the members of the Middelburg Automatic Rifle Club for their support of last Thursday's piano recital at the town hall.

"But it's going slower than we hoped."

Jaap Marais could not be reached for comment as he was dead. ✪

www.hayibo.com

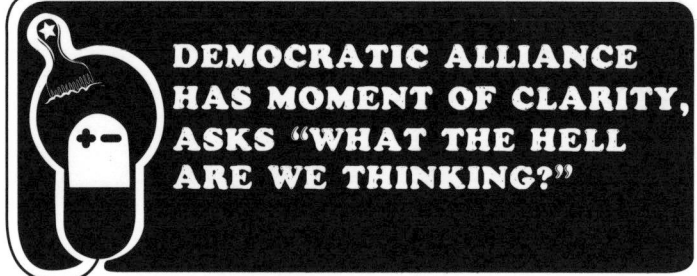
DEMOCRATIC ALLIANCE HAS MOMENT OF CLARITY, ASKS "WHAT THE HELL ARE WE THINKING?"

CAPE TOWN. The Democratic Alliance is to call an extraordinary caucus meeting of senior members to discuss its future, after party leadership admitted that the prospects of a return to white rule in South Africa were "fading fast".

Speaking to reporters outside the DA's Meadowridge compound in Cape Town, spokesperson Nigel Leslie said that DA leader Helen Zille had precipitated the crisis within the party.

"For our year-end bosberaad we usually get together around the log-bar and watch 'The Sound of Music'", explained Leslie. "But this year Ms Zille hired 'Lethal Weapon 2' because she felt that some party members were getting too fond of the lyrics of 'Edelweiss', which mentions being 'small and white, clean and bright', and that we could all do with being reminded about the evils of Apartheid and the debt we owe to Mel Gibson and Danny Glover for helping end it."

Leslie said that the change had brought on a sudden and severe slump in party morale.

"Obviously part of that was the dialogue and editing," he said, "but at the end of it there was generally a sense of 'What the hell are we thinking?'"

According to Leslie, Northern Cape MP Vleis Verwoerd "spoke for everyone" when he pointed out during a session of trust-falls that the DA had two choices: aim to be the opposition, in which case its voters had to commit themselves to being eternal losers; or try to win power, in which case a white person would be running the country.

"It's helluva depressing," said Leslie.

However, he added, the party would try to stay proactive, and to this end was introducing new positions "to reflect more closely the needs of our voters". These include a High Commissioner for Writing Angry Letters to Cape Town Newspapers, a Deputy Madam who will supervise garden labour, and a new media liaison officer, who will need to be able to say "Many of my best friends are black" in at least three South African languages, including English and Afrikaans.

search results related to: lethal weapon 2

ALBINO JOURNALIST HEARTBROKEN AFTER EXCLUSION FROM BLACKS-ONLY FORUM

JOHANNESBURG. While last week's launch of the Forum of Black Journalists continues to draw criticism for its blacks-only segregationist policy, one journalist says he is heartbroken at being booted from the Forum along with his white colleagues. Now albino Jake Mahlangu is asking: "Is it because I is white?"

Mahlangu, who suffers from extreme pigmentation deficiency, says he was shocked when Forum bouncers told him that whites were not welcome in the gathering, where Jacob Zuma was scheduled to present his vision for a non-racial South Africa.

"I know I'm a little bit chalky," said Mahlangu, "but am I not a man and a brother?"

Forum spokesman Idi X said that while the organisation was sorry for any offence caused to Mahlangu, mistakes were bound to happen.

"Discriminating against people on the grounds of their skin colour is an inexact science," he said, adding that the official scrapping of Apartheid-era racial classifications had "muddied the water somewhat for those of us who like to call a spade a spade, and a white reactionary lickspittle a white reactionary lickspittle."

Meanwhile a proposed rival media lobby group, dominated by white journalists and featuring a pro-white bias, has been scrapped.

"We felt that the Forum of Black Journalists couldn't go unanswered," said an unnamed insider this week. "We envisioned a major media house, with disproportionately many white employed, and with a big investment in Afrikaans-language media. News programming would feature a pessimistic, almost despairing tone, and would focus on anonymous crime, corruption in government, and the breakdown of national infrastructure.

"But then we realised that Naspers beat us to it."

search results related to: black as

HOROSCOPE

Scorpio - Oct 24 - Nov 21

You'll win an important argument at work this week. Your colleague will insist that Porky's was the worst film of the 1980s, but history will support you in your claim that it was 'Caddyshack'.

AVERAGE AGE OF DA YOUTH LEAGUE DROPS TO 39

CAPE TOWN. The average age of the Democratic Alliance's Youth League has plunged to 39 after two of its oldest members left the organisation this week. Brad du Plessis, 48, emigrated to Australia, while Mary Jenkins, the Youth League's Treasurer, died peacefully in her sleep, aged 87.

The official opposition has been struggling to shrug off its image as a party for middle-aged white people, and regular attempts to gain youth support have had little success.

2006's 'Rock Music Jamboree for Young Folk' was a conspicuous failure, with just 20 people attending, including ten Youth League veterans, their children, and one grandchild. The following year's event, called 'You're Never Too Old to Bop for Democracy', fared little better, and was called off an hour before the scheduled 10pm close after the deejay ran out of Cliff Richard albums.

However, the party says it is not disheartened, and remains committed to finding youth support.

"I believe the children are our future," said Youth coordinator Crizelda-Marie Smuts. "And there are quite a lot in reformatories and orphanages that would just love a free Democratic Alliance T-shirt and a cup of Oros and a Romany Cream in return for their souls, ag, I mean signatures."

Meanwhile the Youth League's national leadership has sent a telegram of congratulation to its Bloemfontein branch for increasing membership by 100% last year by signing up a Mr Adolph Niemand, 34.

www.hayibo.com

NEW DA PARTY LOGO FEATURES LOTS OF WHITE, NO BLACK

JOHANNESBURG. The newly relaunched Democratic Alliance, desperate to shake off its image as a party for whites, says its new logo is a reflection of how much it has transformed. The logo was revealed on the weekend and features a snow-white sun streaming rays of white light down on a stylized South African landscape that contains no black whatsoever.

The logo's designer, Gladys Riefenstahl, 84, of Squirrel Nutkin Lodge in Brakpan's Casa Blanca Golf and Security Estate, said the dominant white sun and complete absence of black were not indicative of any kind of unconscious racism in herself or the party.

"Some of my best friends use black in their designs," she told media this morning.

"It's a lovely vibrant colour, with great rhythm."

However, she said, black "tended to overwhelm whatever it was introduced to".

The new logo replaces the party's previous motif, which featured a golden sun rising over a blue ocean symbolizing the aspiration of many DA voters to seek a new dawn overseas.

The party confirmed that it will still be known as the Democratic Alliance, but refused to reveal what it was allied with, denying that it had any power-sharing arrangement with either the defunct National Party or its other primary power base, the Arthur Murray School of Dance.

Meanwhile the DA has praised local organizers at its conference for averting a repeat of the unpleasant scenes that have dogged meetings of the newly formed Congress of the People, where ANC members have been accused of breaking up gatherings and intimidating speakers.

According to security consultant Darrel Sundance-Kidd, only a handful of ANC protesters arrived, the rest having been diverted by a rumour of a 25%-off sale at Markham's.

However, he said, those who did arrive outside the conference centre were "efficiently guided to an alternative venue" by trailing life-size cardboard cutouts of Mosiuoa Lekota and Mbhazima Shilowa on string behind a car.

He said that most of the protesters had given up after several dozen kilometres, by which time they had run out of plastic chairs to throw at the cutouts.

search results related to: cardboard cutouts

OTHER BREAKING NEWS

★ **Blackouts back as Eskom caught off guard by shock cooling called "winter"**

★ **Calls for Eskom minister's to resign greeted with loud farts**

www.hayibo.com

VAGINA A MYTH SAY SAUDI SCIENTISTS

RIYADH. The so-called 'vagina' is a myth, and women should stop trying to claim that they enjoy sex, says a group of Saudi grand viziers.

The viziers, all experts in modern Saudi scientific fields such as astrology, water divination and alchemy, were speaking at the launch of their new study, 'Between the Cracks: Stop Fannying About with Our Women', which has set out to prove that the 'vagina' is nothing more than an extension of the buttocks.

"Everybody knows that women are non-sexual creatures," said team leader Prince Abdul Abdul Abdul. "This fantasy about a female sexual organ, this subversive and frankly repulsive idea of a 'vagina', is yet another assault on our values and customs by the West."

Senior researcher Abdul Saud agreed. "Ask any man in the Kingdom if his wife has ever showed the slightest bit of enjoyment while fulfilling the nasty but essential work of spawning a male heir, and he will tell you that sex for women is, and always has been, utterly joyless."

"Until now, we naturally assumed that this lack of pleasure was the fault of the woman partner, perhaps due to some inherent psychological handicap shared by all women," said Grand Vizier of Numerology, Professor Faisal Abdul Saud. "But now we have shown that women are not only stunted psychologically, but physically too."

The team admitted that they had not questioned any actual women during the course of their research, since this would have required having a conversation with one, which is frowned upon in the Saudi scientific community.

Asked if they had ever heard of the clitoris, they confirmed that they had.

"Clitoris was a common name for girl-children in the mid-Victorian era," said Prof. Saud, adding that it sounded quaint and "faintly reminiscent of flowers".

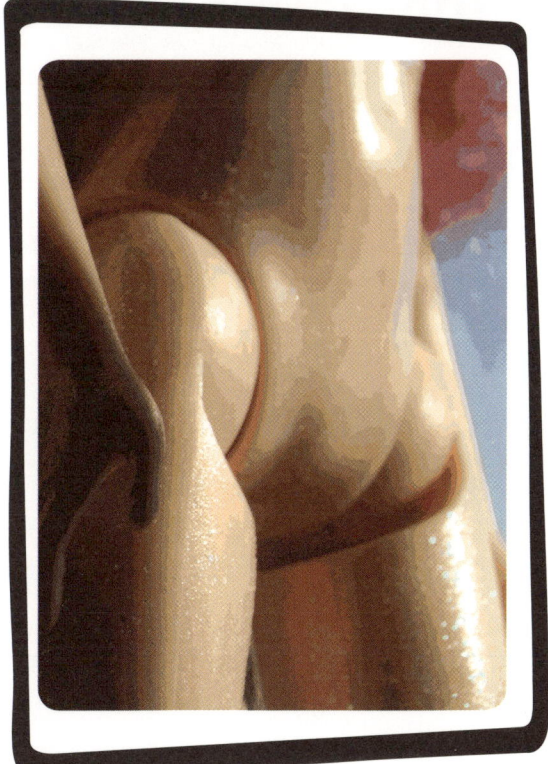

search results related to: vagina myth

OTHER BREAKING NEWS

★ **Second Johannesburg airport just for burning stolen luggage**

★ **Domestic worker responsible for power crisis – Eskom**

★ **Disappointed, malnourished Gautengers remember coast being more fun**

www.hayibo.com

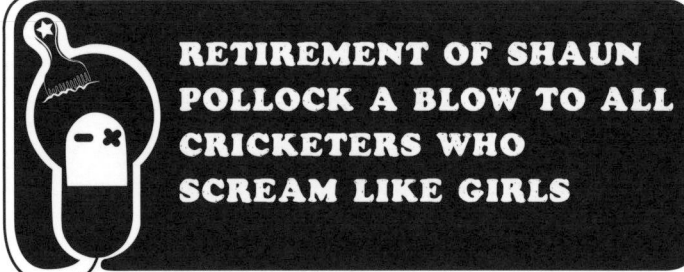

RETIREMENT OF SHAUN POLLOCK A BLOW TO ALL CRICKETERS WHO SCREAM LIKE GIRLS

JOHANNESBURG. Cricketers who scream like girls when their team takes a wicket said goodbye to an icon of the girlish-screaming tradition, as South African star allrounder walked into retirement on Sunday evening.

Pollock, who took over 800 wickets in Test and one-day international cricket, saluted his fans at a packed Wanderers Stadium that will never more ring out with the sound of his girlish whoops and shrieks.

Born in Port Elizabeth in 1973 and first playing for South Africa in 1995, the 'Ginger Ninja' built a lasting legacy as one of the game's great fast bowlers and perhaps its most stunningly effeminate screamer of all time.

Pundits and media figures have been divided over Pollock's form in recent seasons, but on Sunday they were united in their praise for a man who has single-handedly injected a sense of girlish glee into the South African game.

"Polly's contribution is really immeasurable," said The Star's Ahmed Ismael. "Nothing said 'I'm at the cricket' like hearing Polly go 'Whooo-hoo-hoo-hoo!' when he'd just got someone to nick off."

'Sunday Times' veteran Chucky Le Fevre agreed that Pollock had "reinvented the celebratory roar".

"In the early days we just had the likes of Kepler Wessels and Hansie Cronje going 'Raaar!' when a wicket fell. Pollock's falsetto giggle, like a debutante getting felt up behind the bicycle shed, really ushered in a new era for us."

However, Le Fevre expressed concern that Pollock's legacy was not entirely safe.

"I'm not convinced that Graeme Smith is a world-class screamer," he said. "He still comes off as immature, a bit of a Head Boy figure going 'Yaaaaar!' because he's got his Head Girl pregnant."

He added that Jacques Kallis was "shirking his responsibility."

"As a senior player, Jacques should at least be trying to shriek. Obviously there's only one Polly, and clear falsetto voices like that don't come along every day, but when you've got Smith going 'Yaaaaaar!' and Mark Boucher going 'Ah laaaaakit ah laaaaakit boyz!', you just can't afford to have Jacques going 'Zzzzzzz' at first slip."

search results related to: debutante cricketers

Motlanthe collapses after strings cut, ANC mulls new puppet

PRETORIA. South African President Kgalema Motlanthe has been rushed to a private workshop after the strings that move his limbs and keep him upright were accidentally cut. An ANC spokesman also confirmed that his jaw mechanism had also been slightly damaged but said this was not a serious problem as it was not Motlanthe's job to say anything.

Motlanthe had been addressing journalists this morning at a briefing entitled 'Trust Me, I Know What I'm Doing, Mostly' and had just begun to defend his credibility as President when the incident took place.

Shocked onlookers said that Motlanthe had just rattled his little wooden fists on the lectern and stamped his little wooden clogs on the floor, exclaiming, "I'm a real President!" when his strings were cut and he slumped to the floor.

However, ANC spokeswoman Opiate Maponya said that there was no cause for concern.

She said that the cause of the incident was being investigated but that early indications pointed to Deputy President Baleka Mbete, who had been clipping her fingernails while waiting for the President to finish talking.

"We believe Comrade Mbete's grooming regimen may have compromised the strings as they moved across her clippers, at which point Comrade President Motlanthe was redeployed to the floor."

She said that Motlanthe was recovering well but added that the ANC would consider appointing a caretaker puppet to fill in while Motlanthe's jaw was oiled and new strings were attached.

However, she would neither confirm nor deny speculation that the new puppet would be a larger and more sophisticated ventriloquist's dummy and not a traditional wooden puppet.

"We categorically deny the insinuation that traditional puppets are difficult to control," she said. "The Comrades of the National Executive Council have proven themselves masters at all the nuances of puppetry. However, the struggle is constantly evolving and we must evolve with it. If Comrade Zuma believes that the nation would best be served by a ventriloquist President sitting on his knee, then that is his decision."

Meanwhile the office of ANC President Jacob Zuma has confirmed that it has received an official complaint from a group of professional ventriloquists and puppeteers who say that he moves his lips too much when making President Motlanthe perform in public.

However, it assured the group that Zuma's shows would not go on for much longer as he was "planning to ditch the dummies and take over the spotlight as soon as court proceedings allow".

search results related to: Motlanthe puppet

ZILLE TO SEND ARMY AFTER TAXIS, THEN HAIRSTYLIST AND DANCE INSTRUCTOR

CAPE TOWN. Just days after vowing to send the army into Cape Town to crush a threatened strike by taxi bosses, tough mayor and Opposition leader Helen Zille says she will task the South African National Defence Force with hunting down and destroying the people who told her that her hairstyle was fabulous and who taught her a series of hip-hop dance moves.

Zille's threat to use the army to enforce law and order in the ongoing taxi dispute has raised eyebrows, not least within the armed forces, who say they never signed on to do any actual fighting.

According to SANDF spokesperson Brigadier Daisy Makwetla of the 110th Padded Immobile Infantry, the army was reluctant to confront taxi bosses as they were "flipping dangerous".

She added that any kind of major operation in the city would also severely disrupt the SANDF's capacity to continue eating sausage rolls and playing dominoes.

However, this morning Helen Zille's spokesman, Thabo Token-Black, confirmed that the Cape Town mayor was determined to see justice prevail.

"Obviously with the election so close we don't want to make any alarmist statements," said Token-Black. "But I don't think it would be out of line to suggest that taxi owners are about to meet with Helen's good friend, Pain."

He confirmed that she was also briefing military commanders about a potential surgical strike against her hairstylist and a freelance dance instructor named Faisal.

"Nobody wants to point fingers, least of all us," he explained. "But you've seen the footage of the hair and the dancing. People need to die."

Asked what the DA's message to voters would be over the next few weeks, Token-Black said that it would be a message of respect and tolerance.

"Except for Maurice of Hackles Glam Parlour. And his little dog. And Faisal, who said he could turn Helen into Fergie from the Black Eyed Peas in three sessions. And Faisal's homey Abdol who told Helen that the hip-hop hand wave would look totally bitchin'.

"They need to run and hide, because there's a world of hurt coming their way. Helen's coming to kick ass and chew bubblegum, and she's all out of gum."

Zille could not be reached for further comment as she had reportedly taken the DA's senior leadership on a twenty-mile forced march on thorns to "root out the weak and fling their carcasses to the jackals", or to ask them to resign, whichever seemed more appropriate at the time.

www.hayibo.com

WORLD BEGS STEVEN SEAGAL TO END CHINESE CRACKDOWN IN TIBET

GENEVA. As outrage grows over China's heavy-handed crackdown on Tibetan protesters, world leaders have issued a unified call on Buddhist fighting machine Steven Seagal to intervene in the crisis, urging him to "summon the speed of the puma and the strength of the bison so that he can kick Chinese ass."

Speaking at an emergency summit in Geneva, German chancellor Angela Merkel told reporters that only Seagal had the necessary skills required to force China to back down.

"Many people are asking us why we haven't approached someone like Chuck Norris," said Merkel, acknowledging Norris's "stellar record when it comes to rescuing women from cages in the Mekong Delta."

She said that the decision would have been more difficult had Chinese authorities begun rounding up attractive Tibetan women and putting them in cages in the Mekong Delta.

However, she said, Seagal had been a unanimous choice once it became clear that Beijing had opted for more conventional oppression, assault and abduction.

"Steven brings an oriental gravitas to his violence that Mr Norris lacks," said British Prime Minister Gordon Brown. "Like all intrinsically cruel and cunning civilizations, the Chinese respect understatement. Steven is nothing if not understated.

"Plus he is also dead good-looking. Some people say he is fat, but that's like racism against fat people."

French president Nicolas Sarkozy said that delegates at the summit had been particularly encouraged by the fact that Seagal seemed to have his own Asian wardrobe, and would not need to be specially fitted for robes, silk slippers or ninja toe-socks.

Seagal could not be reached for comment as he was talking to the wind in western Nepal, but his agent confirmed that he had received the summit's call for help, and was meditating on it.

"When you're a fighting mystic minstrel there's a lot you need to process," she said. "Also he needs to figure out how much ammunition to take. There's something like four billion Chinese. That's a lot of shooting, even for Steven."

search results related to: buddhist fighting machine

MBEKI LEGACY INTACT, SAYS MBEKI

DARFUR. Thabo Mbeki says only history can judge his legacy, and if history judges him critically then history is a racist. Speaking to journalists in Sudan where he is currently trying to negotiate a ceasefire between rival gangs of feral goatherds, Mbeki said that even if he were fired by the ANC he would walk away with his integrity and his pension intact.

The South African President faces an uncertain future after Judge Chris "Chopper" Nicholson implicated Mbeki in a political conspiracy against ANC president Jacob Zuma, and many party stalwarts are calling for his head while having to explain to Julius Malema that they don't want Mbeki's actual head.

According to insiders, the ANC has gone as far as saying that it wants to confiscate the presidential hairball.

The hairball, removed from the stomach of a cow, was bought by Mbeki from an online store of esoteric artefacts, and reportedly allows him to see the future and interpret current events.

An aide in the Presidency who asked to remain anonymous confirmed that the hairball is consulted almost daily.

"Mr Mbeki puts on a special wig, and then rubs the hairball against Essop Pahad's tummy, blows on it, and then presses it to his ear," he said.

He also confirmed that Mbeki's policies on Aids, xenophobia, education, crime prevention and weapons procurements were all suggested by the hairball.

Presidency staff have also confirmed that they have started shredding the 1.7 million pages of text Mbeki has written while in office. According to the staffers, the documents, mostly variations on a theme of paranoia, will be turned into confetti and rained down on Jacob Zuma when he enters the Presidency.

Meanwhile a spokesman for Mbeki said that the President would go about his peacekeeping duties untroubled by events in South Africa.

"Mr Mbeki remains fully focused on sorting out the Al-Haqadi grazing rights dispute here in Darfur," said Macduff Maponyane. "He has always had the ability to blank out public opinion when he needs to, thanks largely to the fact that he does not particularly care what South Africans think, feel, or want."

According to Maponyane, Mbeki was confident that history would vindicate his actions as president, largely thanks to a new history textbook, written by Mbeki, that would be prescribed in all South African schools next year.

search results related to: presidential hairball

AUSTRALIANS CELEBRATE ETHNIC DIVERSITY

CANBERRA. Australians of all ethnic groups have come together to mark Australian Diversity Day, celebrating the country's rich history and diverse ethnic heritage. According to government organizers, special attention is being given to Australia's native tribes – the Welsh, the Scots, the Irish, the Northern Irish, the southern Welsh, and the Highland Scots.

Asked if Aborigines were being included in ADD celebrations, spokesman Russell Dag said he would not "respond to the f****ing Spanish Inquisition of the politically correct asking f***king subversive questions".

However, he confirmed that the nation's Aborigines had been invited to join celebrations in Canberra, on condition that they paid for their own bus tickets, promised to use cutlery at the reception, and refrained from "doing any of that creepy Dreamtime song-and-dance bullshit" in their motel rooms. He said the invitation had been declined.

He added that the "continued childish standoffishness of the Aboriginalese" was a source of pain and frustration for the government, despite its best efforts to improve the Aborigines' lot by "teaching their children the value of a good forward defensive and how to spot a well-flighted googly".

"We are deeply disappointed that they have chosen not to join us in celebration of the great melting pot that is Australia, where vanilla ice-cream melts together with white chocolate, icing sugar, coconut milk, and a bit of salt." However, he said, officials did not want "a small bunch of cry-babies daubing shitty paintings of shitty lizards on shitty rocks" to spoil the day for those "who made Australia what it is".

The slogan of Australian Diversity Day is 'Australia: A Home for All, Even Asians', and Dag said his government was proud of Australia's history of being a place of refuge for the oppressed.

"Throughout the history of mankind, this country has opened her arms to lost souls from all over the world seeking to make a new life on her sun-kissed shores," he said. He later conceded that "throughout the history of mankind" referred to the latter part of the 18th century, and that "from all over the world" referred specifically to the northern British Isles.

"But it's the thought that counts, you f***wits," he told journalists.

ZIMBABWE SAYS CONTINENTAL DRIFT IS BRITISH PLOT

HARARE. Continental drift is a plot by Britain, say the African country's leading thinkers, who have accused Downing Street of "systematically inching the depraved colonizing cesspool away from Zimbabweans who want to go and live there."

The geological phenomenon was first identified by the Zimbabwean Minister for Arts and Culture, Brigadier Napoleon Sunshine Moyo, in 2001.

"I parked my car outside my office in the morning, and when I returned, my car was parked in the neighbouring bay," Moyo told the media at the time. "It had shifted about three metres to the left.

"It was a very jolly thing to discover."

Harare Police Department investigators tried to convince Moyo that the car he had found was in fact his secretary's, and that his own car had been stolen and subsequently found 17 kilometres away in a ditch, but Moyo would have none of it, declaring their protests "anti-scientific and probably racist in origin".

His findings were formalized in a scientific journal the following year, and continental drift has since been known as the Moyo Effect in Zimbabwe.

This week the Minister's discovery was back in the spotlight, as a spokesman for the Presidency, Breakfast Nkala, told reporters that the gradual shift of the earth's tectonic plates was "a typically provocative bid from Tony Blair to prevent Zimbabweans from protesting the colonizer's abuse of honest Africans by leaving honest Africa and going to live on the dole in south London."

When asked if he knew that Tony Blair was no longer Prime Minister, Nkala responded that he was "not interested in Western lies".

He added that the "desperate geological retreat by Blair the puppet-master" would be keenly felt by Zimbabwean academia. Every year approximately 100 Zimbabwean students, largely the children of senior Zanu-PF politicians, enrol in English tertiary institutions: last year Meatballs Taibu, son of prominent minister Hotlips Meatballs Taibu, became the first Zimbabwean to complete a Master's degree at the Oxfordshire Agricultural College, where he excelled in pottery, voodoo, and denial.

Moyo said that while the Mugabe government was not yet sure just how Gordon Brown was moving the earth's crust, it suspected "racist hydraulics".

Downing Street has denied being responsible for continental drift, but has expressed some interest in the concept of racist hydraulics as a possible way of keeping Poles and Romanians out of Britain. ✪

search results related to: zim parking lot

SURVEY

The Independent Democrats have found a killer on their Election list. They should:

◯ Let him run, they could hardly do any worse

◯ Fire him, even if it means they've now only got 19 members

◯ Subcontract him out to Julius "Metaphorical" Malema on weekends

◯ Let him run because he represents thousands of South Africans

www.hayibo.com

AUSTRALIA TELLS ABORIGINES THE CHEQUE IS IN THE MAIL

LAST HONEST PUBLIC OFFICIAL TO AUCTION INTEGRITY TO HIGEST BIDDER

CANBERRA. Just days after presenting what has been hailed as an 'almost completely sincere-sounding apology' to Australia's Aborigines, the country's Prime Minister has announced that his government has posted tribal elders a cheque for $367.52 after sending a hat around Parliament.

"At the moment the cheque is in the mail," said the PM's spokesperson Dingo McShane, "but when it arrives, I expect it will bring some cheer into those dusty, dusky little hearts of theirs."

McShane said that the decision to send a hat around Parliament had caused an uproar, with many lawmakers suggesting that the money would be squandered on "firewater and those tennis sweatbands they wear".

However, in a compromise move the legislature agreed to send the money as well as "some goodies they really need out there on the reservations, like pants, shampoo and conditioner, and Shane Warne's autobiography."

"We feel the money was important," said McShane. "Give a man to fish, and you feed him for a day. Teach a man to fish, and he'll empty the bloody rivers faster than you can say 'Kyoto'. At least if you give him a fish he's taken care of for today. Tomorrow we'll renegotiate."

Meanwhile the administration has vowed to tackle rampant alcoholism in aboriginal communities. "Our door is always open," said McShane. "If any tribal elder wants to come in and discuss the issue of alcohol abuse, I'd be happy to discuss it over a couple of pints." ○

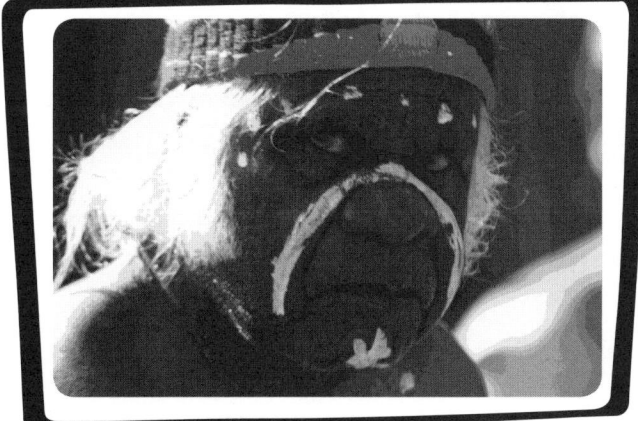

search results related to: dinkum white devils

ALICE. The last remaining honest public official in South Africa, Mr Godknows Mkhize of the Alice municipality, says he has had enough of earning an honest living while all the country's other public servants enrich themselves without fear of being caught or fired. Mr Mkhize has confirmed that he will auction his integrity to the highest bidder sometime this week.

According to a study conducted by only marginally corrupt analysts, South Africa boasted a total of four honest public officials in 2008.

However, two of them were found with passport-manufacturing machinery in their cars earlier this year, while the third, who had threatened to expose graft in his department, accidentally shot himself in the back nine times from a nearby rooftop while cleaning his sniper's rifle.

A delighted Mr Mkhize was quoted at the time as saying that he was proud to be the only honest public servant in the country, and that he would try hard to keep working long hours for a pitiful salary while his colleagues snorted lines of cocaine off the buttocks of models in the cubicle next door.

But this morning he admitted that he was "sick and tired" of being honest. "I want what they have," he told journalists from his desk at the Alice municipality. "The snorting and the buttocks and whatnot."

He said that he could not afford cocaine as he had not yet been corrupted, but said he would snort lines of snuff or icing sugar until he "scored some sweet little tender deal".

"Nothing hectic," he explained. "Just something where I get a brown envelope once a week and half a sheep now and then." He said that his long-term goal was to be caught with his hand in the till and suspended on full pay.

"That's the new South African dream," he mused. "It's what every little kid wants nowadays. When I was young I wanted to be an astronaut. Now my boy wants to be a local government councillor suspended on full pay."

Meanwhile the government has denied that the 16.3 million public servants currently suspended on full pay are harming the economy. Speaking at the launch of a new government department that will fast-track the sale of state land to old friends, the issuing of tenders to family members and the accidental incineration of police dockets, spokesman Caligula Nyamende said that taxpayers had nothing to fear.

"Those public servants who have been suspended on full pay mostly spend their days texting their friends and chewing bubblegum, which was pretty much all they did while they were working for the state. "So in that way nothing has changed," he explained. ○

www.hayibo.com

OUTCOMES-BASED MATRICS DECONSTRUCT RESULTS, REJECT COLONIAL ALPHABET

PRETORIA. The first South African school-leavers to write the same national outcomes-based examination have deconstructed their results, acknowledging historically unjust grading systems while examining their own emotional response to completing a discovery-based secondary education. However, those polled did not know which letter came after D.

Speaking to journalists this morning, Deputy Education Minister Xoliswa Seespot-Runn congratulated the country's 600,000 matriculants on their results, which she said was evidence that most candidates had managed to find examination venues and figured out how to open question papers and orient them the right way up.

"That is a triumph in itself," she said. "Outcomes-based learning is all about self-discovery, so it is wonderful that our learners have reached a level where they know which end of a pencil to hold."

She also praised teachers for embracing the ethos of outcomes-based teaching.

"OBE is not about being prescriptive or telling people what to think, or indeed how to think.

"Thanks to our dedicated cadre of teachers, who have told their learners nothing about anything, our young people have been left entirely alone to work out answers for themselves.

"This has translated into the most wonderful and creative answers to exam questions. For instance, one candidate proved that 3 times 4 equals porridge. That's exactly the kind of lateral thinking we want to encourage."

Asked why 97 percent of those who passed the exam did not know which letter came after D in the alphabet, Seespot-Runn said that the alphabet was considered a colonial and prescriptive tool of mental oppression.

"Also nobody gets an E any more," she added. "If we see a learner struggling, there is a wonderful educational tool called Microsoft Excel, where you just press a button on a spreadsheet and all the marks round up to the nearest 50 percent."

Meanwhile the country's top pupils spent the day celebrating by locking themselves in their bedrooms and sobbing for two hours while trying to understand a numb sense of anticlimax after twelve years of anxiety.

The top achiever in the country was Chrizelda-Marie-Sunette-Chantay van Blerk of Pretoria's Christelike Hoërskool vir Vervelige Meisiekinders, who achieved 103 percent in each of her nine subjects.

Chrizelda-Marie-Sunette-Chantay was unavailable for comment as she was in her bedroom sobbing uncontrollably while staring into the abyss that was the rest of her life, but her parents Vleis and Omo told journalists that her favourite subjects had been Parental Pressure Orientation, Middle-Class Aspirational Studies, and Blind Ambition. ✪

search results related to: colonial education

SURVEY

Kgalema Motlanthe reportedly has a young Mistress. That's:

◯ Scandalous. As President he should only be screwing taxpayers

◯ Brilliant! At last! Evidence of a soul!

◯ No biggie. All the best Presidents are doing it nowadays

www.hayibo.com

MORGAN FREEMAN TO BE NELSON MANDELA FOR FORESEEABLE FUTURE

LOS ANGELES. Veteran actor Morgan Freeman will be Nelson Mandela for the foreseeable future. A South African government stylist said that the liberation icon was still fully alert and fit, but added that "the whole doddery granddad thing is very 1990s".

Mandela, who spent 27 years in prison so that Bob Geldof and Bono could sell more albums, turns 90 in July, and many within the ruling African National Congress party believe that it is time for the former president to become Morgan Freeman.

Speaking to film producers, stylists, and party stalwarts, ANC spokesman Bheki Tswete said Mr Mandela had been a "saviour for three generations of mediocre pop stars, bored British liberals, T-shirt manufacturers and tour guides".

"Madiba broke rocks on Robben Island so that we could all make money from the 46664 brand," said Tswete.

However, he said, the demands being placed on the ageing statesman required that he become a younger, more attractive man.

"Morgan Freeman seemed the obvious choice," said official ANC stylist Hotlips Hlope. "He's got the cheekbones, he's got the gravitas, but most of all he can do that beautiful quasi-African accent, like he did when he played Nazeem in 'Robin Hood: Prince of Thieves'."

According to sources in Pretoria, Freeman's official duties will include "looking regal, saying 'What curious ways you have, Christian' in his Nazeem voice, and doing that crazy little Madiba dance."

Tswete would neither confirm nor deny that Freeman had caused a diplomatic row by saying that Mandela's famous side-to-side dance looked "like the Tin Woodman from 'The Wizard of Oz' trying to shake a suppository loose."

However, he did confirm that Freeman has offered to update the dance with a quick two-step and a heel-clicking jump.

"We told him that Mr Mandela was not Mr Bojangles," said Tswete. "To the best of my knowledge his dog has not yet up and died."

Meanwhile Freeman has said that he is delighted to be taking up his new post as Nelson Mandela, and that he "can't wait" to say 'What curious ways you have, Christian' at White House banquets.

search results related to: nelson freeman

OTHER BREAKING NEWS

★ **ANC meets to test how inept it can be before voters abandon it**

★ **More lies as Carl Niehaus admits he is divorced mother of four**

★ **St Patrick's Day passes, world remembers Irish are still just loud bog people**

www.hayibo.com

US MARINES SEE BLINDING LIGHT ON ROAD TO DAMASCUS

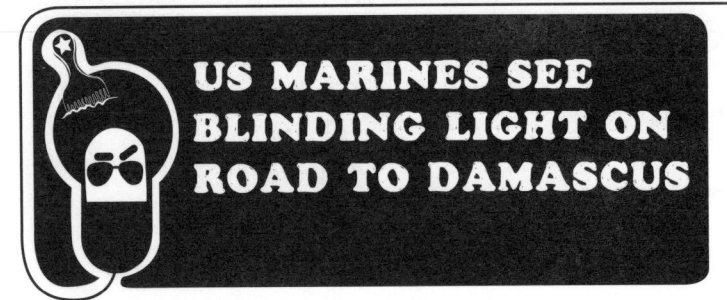

BAGHDAD. A platoon of the 101st Airborne Division is being debriefed in a military hospital inside Baghdad's Green Zone after being thrown off their transporter by what the Pentagon has described as "a blinding light on the road to Damascus." Some of the men are being treated for second-degree burns.

"At this time it's difficult to ascertain whether it was a roadside bomb or in fact, as is being suggested by the White House, an apparition by the Lord God Almighty," Pentagon spokesperson Colonel Mitchell Johnson said late yesterday.

However, he added that neither possibility was being ruled out.

"Without better intel, whether ballistic or theological, we simply can't make a call on this one," said Johnson.

"For example, we need to determine whether or not God can manifest as a landmine, and if He can, why He would go that route instead of opting for something more biblical, like a burning bush pumping out some sort of napalm."

Johnson confirmed that Pentagon experts were also divided over the issue of God's loyalty.

"A lot of high-level analysts are raising the issue of treason," he said, adding that it is common knowledge in the US that God was born in Idaho, and educated at the West Point military academy.

"We're not saying He couldn't knock over a Humvee if He wanted to, but again, we're wondering why, given His Methodist upbringing, He would want to."

However, he said he would not be drawn on whether he thought God had drifted away from His traditional allies, and had found a new Chosen People, such as the Swedes or the French.

"We're staying pragmatic," said Johnson. "At this time we're sticking with the land-mine hypothesis. Now all we need to clear up is whether He would deploy as shrapnel, or go with the more conventional payload of white doves and dew."

Johnson said he could confirm that no white doves had been seen at the site, and that a clear liquid found on one soldier, initially thought to be fresh mountain dew, was in fact fresh Mountain Dew. ✪

HILLARY EDGES AHEAD OF RIVAL AS PERSON AMERICANS WOULD LEAST LIKE TO SEE NAKED

WASHINGTON DC. Embattled Democratic contender Hillary Clinton is one step closer to being named as the person Americans would be most traumatized by seeing in the nude. According to insiders, her uncomfortable body language and "creepily stringy" appearance have nudged her ahead of challenger Michael Moore.

Early polling last week suggested that filmmaker Moore was headed for a comfortable win, with his trademark stubbly jowls and open-toe sandals consistently appalling voters from all population groups.

However, this week's two point lead for the former First Lady confirmed a growing suspicion that Americans are increasingly finding lean elderly flesh more nauseating than grotesquely distended blubber.

Speaking to the media at the publication of the poll results, pollster Gerald Pendergrass said at the heart of the shift was trust.

"On the one hand you've got a guy who's not pretty. He's big, he looks like he might be smelly, and yes, you'll blow chunks if you accidentally see him in the shower.

"But there are shared values there. You probably take the same diabetes medication. There's love.

"And then there's Hillary. You just know that if you bumped into her with her kit off it would be like seeing a human-sized lampshade made out of tanned skin. It's Hannibal Lecter stuff, seriously."

Pendergrass agreed that looking like a collection of dissected corpses spread over a lamp by a serial killer could be a hindrance to Clinton's presidential aspirations, but added that it wasn't necessarily a body blow to her campaign.

"John F. Kennedy had a neck that looked like a meatloaf tied up with string, and yet he pulled chicks," said Pendergrass. "There's no reason Hillary can't pull chicks either, if she puts her mind to it." ✪

HOROSCOPE

Libra - 22 Sep - 22 Oct

Remember that your body is a temple. It's time to kick out the moneylenders, but be careful not to punch a rabbi in the mouth.

www.hayibo.com

NINTENDO LAUNCHES WII SEX CONSOLE

NEW YORK. Gaming giant Nintendo has unveiled its latest offering in the handheld console market, the Wii Sex. Launching the fully interactive digital sex simulation, a company spokesman said, "It is extremely unlikely that anyone who uses a Wii has ever had, or will ever have, sex, so this is a perfect opportunity to introduce them to the joys of lovemaking."

The new console, which was presented to the media at Nintendo's Manhattan headquarters this morning, measures just over six inches in length and sports a rosy knob on the end.

Spokesman Stan Flintlock told gathered journalists that the company believed Wii Sex would fit snugly into a niche in the market.

"We know our consumers, and we know that they aren't having sex," he said.

"In fact, they're not really having any physical contact of any sort with other people."

However, he said, it was this gaming culture that would underpin the future success of Wii Sex.

"What is the one thing that all experienced gamers are good at doing?

"The answer is obvious: playing with themselves.

"That's all gamers do. They play with themselves all day long. So what better way to introduce them to the exquisite, private pleasures of sex than with an animated partner of their choice, taking flat-screen passion to the limit?"

Critics of the gaming industry have long insisted that the Wii – a sensory device that translates physical action into digital game-play – is undermining international efforts to get children and young adults to take up physical activity to help fight obesity.

But Flintlock pre-empted criticism of Wii Sex, saying that as a middle-aged games enthusiast he could testify to the fact that some sex, however lonely and awkward it would inevitably be given the constraints of the console, was better than none at all.

"Waving your arm around can get really tiring," he said. "Research has shown that if you flex your wrist nine hours a day for 34 years, you can burn the same amount of fat you would lose running half a marathon."

Asked if Wii Sex would be marketed to non-traditional gamers and people who have had sex at least once, Flintlock said that a wider audience would definitely be targeted.

"We've already convinced a lot of sensible non-gamers that Wii can be used as an exercise device. That's like selling crack to moms to use as a milk formula.

"If they'll buy that, they'll buy anything." ★

search results related to: playing with yourself

www.hayibo.com

 ESKOM ASKS PUBLIC TO BE PATIENT, NEEDS MORE TIME TO CONSTRUCT NEW LIES

PRETORIA. Embattled energy provider Eskom says it will need at least six to eight months to construct newer and more convincing lies than the ones it has been using so far.

This morning a spokesman asked the South African public to be patient, adding that affirmative action had led to a severe shortage of qualified and experienced corporate liars.

Some industry experts first cried foul as long ago as January 2006 when massive outages around the country were blamed on birds defecating on powerlines. However, their accusations – that Eskom was employing substandard liars – were largely ignored.

But after two years and countless blackouts the power utility has been forced to admit that its lies have become "increasingly transparent."

"The old 'loose bolt in the generator' was probably the best of a bad bunch," spokesman Eddie Motsepe told journalists in Megawatt Park this morning.

He said that subsequent lies, including fictions about stopping power exports to neighbouring countries, wet coal supplies and why executive bonuses have been deserved, were often "last-minute, late-night efforts" cobbled together at senior management level after young and inexperienced liars had failed to supply the necessary fabrications on time.

"For example, during January's load-shedding, we asked our team to provide us with three plausible lies explaining the blackouts.

"What we got was: 'It was Apartheid what did it', 'My dog at my substation', and 'My granny died and so everyone at Eskom had to go home to the Ciskei for the funeral'.

"Clearly these were not up to industry standard."

Motsepe said that affirmative action and employment equity had been a "major challenge".

"Those guys who learned to lie under the Nationalist regime, those guys were superb," he said. "But we are looking forward, and we believe that with the right guidance, and the country's current atmosphere of corporate denial, unfettered greed and zero accountability, we can get new capacity on stream very soon."

Senior management was not available for comment as its granny had died and it had been forced to go home to the Ciskei for the funeral.

search results related to: lies

HOROSCOPE

Leo Jul 23 - Aug 22 July

Don't be discouraged by the negativity of your friends. Just because your one true love gave you a fake phone number, took his/her name out of the phonebook, got a restraining order and bought a gun, it doesn't mean he/she doesn't see a future with you. One day you'll make them all see that. Even if it means using violence.

www.hayibo.com

SA TO GET NEW PUBLIC HOLIDAY CELEBRATING PUBLIC HOLIDAYS

PRETORIA. Not enough South Africans are taking time to reflect on the vital role public holidays have played in building a democratic society, says a new report commissioned by the state. The government has responded by vowing to fight this growing apathy by instituting a new public holiday, Public Holiday Day.

The report's authors said that public holidays had become "an integral part of who we are as South Africans."

"The five-day working week represents the brutality of Apartheid, where workers were often expected to put in eight hours a day for five days in a row," they told journalists at the Union Buildings.

"No society can function like this, and the 87 annual public holidays that have been created since 1994 have helped to develop a much more groovy work ethic."

However, they said, since 1994 there had been a steady decline in people's awareness of what public holidays meant to the country as a whole.

"Last year we found that a shocking 86 percent of South Africans failed to feel Good Will on the Day of Good Will," said the authors.

"Likewise, only 51 percent of our citizens were women on Women's Day."

They were confident that Public Holiday Day would boost awareness in coming years.

"It's easy to sit back and to think that someone else will take responsibility for observing National Plaque Prevention Day or The Day of Traditional Savoury Recipes," they said.

"After all, when you've just done your shopping for the Day of the Release of the Martyr Tony Yengeni, why would you feel obliged to observe Jacob Zuma's fourth Fifth Wedding Anniversary?

"Clearly our people need to understand that by being diligently slothful, they are advancing the cause of democracy."

ZIMBABWE POLICE READY TO DEFEND DEMOCRACY IN SATURDAY'S POLL

HARARE. Zimbabwe's police say they are ready to defend democracy at all costs during Saturday's election, even if it means shooting voters or blowing up polling stations. Police chief Papsmear Motombo says his officers have also been thoroughly briefed on how to avoid embarrassing incidents. "You shoot the reporters first," he told observers.

International monitors have been concerned in recent days about the number of police being deployed around polling stations, but Motombo explained that Zimbabwe's voters have nothing to fear.

"The torch of democracy needs help to remain alight. If we intervene, it will only be to keep that guttering light a-flicker."

He said this could be done with kerosene, incendiary tracer bullets, and, in some cases, napalm.

Motombo also promised police assistance at polling stations around the country. This would include two officers in each booth, checking that voters have made a mark next to Robert Mugabe's name and filled in multiple duplicates in the same way; and a sound-proofed police caravan in which voters would confirm their names, addresses and pension numbers.

He said these checks were "essential in a democratic context, in case we find irregularities in voting and need to revisit certain spur-of-the-moment voting decisions."

Asked if he expected many spoiled ballots, Motombo said that they were part of any election in Zimbabwe.

"Yes, there are always thousands of spoiled ballots," he said. "Usually it is from blood or brain fluid. It makes the ink run, you see."

Search results related to: zimbabwe voting

www.hayibo.com

PRESSURE ON OBAMA TO THREATEN MUSLIM COUNTRY WITH EXTREME DESTRUCTION

WASHINGTON. After Hillary Clinton's vow that the United States under her presidency would 'obliterate' Iran if it attacked an American ally, rival Barack Obama is under pressure to come up with his own vengeful, ultra-violent threat against a major Middle Eastern country. "He's got to go nuclear, probably against Saudi Arabia," said analysts.

This morning an Obama advisor conceded that they might have underestimated the extent of Clinton's murderous megalomania.

"She'll really do it," said Obama aide Chutney Du Pont. "We weren't sure. We thought this might have been the result of some sort of domestic row with Bill.

"You know how it goes: he wants to go bowling on election night, she calls his loyalty into question, he asks her if she's harping on the Monica thing, she says 'Well don't I have a right to if I want?' and he's like, 'Give it a bone, woman!' and she's like, 'That's right! I'm just a little woman! A little woman with cruise-missiles, bitch!'

"And then she tells him she's going to obliterate Iran, before she makes him sleep on the couch.

"But she means it. It's scary."

According to analysts, Clinton's sabre-rattling statement has left the nuclear ball squarely in Obama's court, and Americans are now waiting to see if the Democrat contender can match her warmongering rhetoric.

"He's got to show he's as keen as Hillary on the mass destruction of Muslims, or risk losing the nomination," said political analyst Leonard Hutch. "It's really tough for him, because 'obliterate' is such a great word. The synonyms just don't sound as good."

According to Hutch, the only real option remaining open to Obama was to promise to "incinerate Saudi Arabia".

"You could opt for the old 'annihilate Malaysia' line, but the problem there is that 'annihilate' sounds a little effeminate; and Malaysia isn't really a threat, plus the people are really good-looking, and they have orangutans, which are endangered."

He said if everything else failed, Obama could "always fall back on vowing to 'really hurt Yemen'." ★

search results related to: obama nuke

SURVEY

After stealing another $90,000 from Zimbabwe's foreign reserves to go on holiday, Grace Mugabe needs to be:

◯ Reminded of how Marie Antoinette was shortened by about a foot

◯ Shortened by about a foot

◯ Sat down and asked if she thinks her life is going in the right direction

◯ Dangled from her Manolo Blahniks until it all falls out of her pockets

22

www.hayibo.com

CRISIS FOR 2010 PLANNERS AFTER SLICK BEIJING OPENING CEREMONY RAISES BAR

JOHANNESBURG. South African football officials say they will have to rethink the planned opening ceremony of the 2010 World Cup after seeing the standard set by the opening of the Beijing Olympics on Friday. This morning worried planners conceded that their blueprints "may have been too heavily reliant on PJ Powers and helium-filled balloons shaped like footballs".

The Beijing extravaganza was watched by over 1.4 billion people, including 1.3 billion Chinese, as well as hundreds of Tibetan dissidents in Chinese prisons whose eyelids were stapled to their foreheads to allow them an uninterrupted view of the festivities.

International commentators have been effusive in their praise, with many Western media figures agreeing that the long rows of Chinese girls in short dresses and white go-go boots who lined the track had forced them to re-evaluate their opinion of China's human rights records.

However, the ceremony came as a severe blow to the team tasked with organising the opening of the 2010 World Cup, who said that there would be "some tough weeks ahead, with a lot of difficult phone calls to a lot of disappointed mimes and beauty pageant runners-up who thought they were going to get their moment in the sun".

The tender for producing the opening ceremony was won in 2006 by Mzansi Empowerment Dynamos, a BEE-compliant company specialising in construction, catering, traditional medicines, textbook publishing, and human waste removal.

CEO Charity Mokwena, a hairdresser who moonlighted as a school inspector before being suspended to give her more time to pursue business interests in the pharmaceuticals and undertaking industries, said that the Beijing spectacle had been "a shock".

"We were pretty sure it would be animal-themed, like the way we do it in South Africa," she said.

"We were absolutely certain they'd have some pandas, maybe led around the stadium on a chain, or on a balancing ball, and then maybe follow up with a big float celebrating Chinese food, like a 20-metre chunk of sweet-and-sour pork floating in the sky.

"That's how we would have done it."

But she said that the show, and its overwhelmingly positive response, had persuaded her that she and her team were on the wrong track with their designs.

"In a nutshell we were looking at about fifteen Zulu dancers doing the whole furry ankle-bracelet stomping thing, and then PJ Powers singing a ballad called 'My African Soul Swells like a Soccer Ball Being Pumped Up', and then about a hundred little kids releasing balloons filled with helium, and then a kid in a wheelchair releasing a white dove."

She said that they were still trying to source a mechanised wheelchair that was impervious to dove faeces.

"We did a test run and the bird crapped on the chair and short-circuited it.

"For some reason it pushed up the revs into the red, and locked the steering on full left turn.

"That poor little kid was basically doing donuts until she blacked out and fell off into some bushes."

She added that the new designs would "probably focus on animals, maybe with elephants playing soccer to symbolise something about something, maybe" ★

OTHER BREAKING NEWS

★ **2010 stadium panic as architects admit Foozball-scale planning**

★ **Resignation of soccer coach shatters SA's World Cup early exit hopes**

★ **Robben Island to woo tourists by stopping being total crap**

www.hayibo.com

GOVERNMENT CONFIRMS MDLADLANA NOT RACIST, JUST VERY STUPID

PRETORIA. The South African government has defended Labour Minister Membathisi Mdladlana, saying his comments about Chinese citizens did not reflect that he was racist but rather that he was "medically an imbecile". It conceded that Mdladlana had been "completely unhinged" since well before he declared Zimbabwe's 2005 election to be free and fair.

This week Mdladlana raised the ire of opposition parties and human rights bodies by demanding Chinese citizens stop speaking Chinese now that they have been reclassified as coloured.

The minister was widely quoted in the press as saying, "They can speak Chinese, of course, in their homes. I have absolutely no difficulty with that. But when we visit them, they must also remember that they are now coloureds. What I know is that coloureds don't speak Chinese."

Speaking to journalists at the Union Buildings, government spokesman Bokkom Kiewiets said that Mdladlana could not be blamed for any racial stereotyping, as he had "the mental capacity of a golden retriever".

"He understands all sorts of commands," said Kiewiets. "'Sit!', 'Stay!', 'Roll over', 'Don't criticize Mugabe!' That sort of thing.

"Where he runs into trouble is when he has to make reasoned judgements about things like racial classification, linguistic trends, tying his shoelaces, or touching his fingertip to his nose with one eye shut."

He said Mdladlana's stint as leader of South Africa's election observer mission to Zimbabwe in 2005 had convinced the government that Mdladlana was "not the sharpest tool in the shed", but that this had not been a problem as "Cabinet was pretty much full of blunt tools, and we needed someone in a suit with wet cement between the ears to rubber-stamp the whole thing for Comrade Robert".

He added Mdladlana would not be available to answer the media's questions as he was busy having applesauce sponged off his bib, and was then scheduled to be bathed by the Speaker of Parliament, powdered by his Director-General, and put to bed by the National Executive Committee.

Meanwhile a delegation of Chinese-speaking coloureds has demanded an apology from the minister.

"If Mdladlana wants to deal in stereotypes, we'll give him a stereotype," said the delegation's spokesman, Denzil February-Wang, of Shanghai Villas, Lotus River.

According to February-Wang, his study group had intended to spend this week in Confucian contemplation, with a short time out to take their grannies to the salon.

"But if he wants to come with this whole 'coloureds are such-and-such' plak, we'll be happy to pick him up in a pimped-out Ford Cortina with wild horses airbrushed on the bonnet, threaten to stab him, blow tik smoke up his nose, bite him with a gold tooth, take him to church with Mommy and Granny, then watch a Manchester United game on Granny's television, and then threaten to stab him again." ✪

BENNY HINN PERFORMED MIRACLE IN, JOHANNESBURG SAY EXPERTS

JOHANNESBURG. Religious and scientific experts say there is strong evidence that American televangelist Benny Hinn performed a "genuine verifiable miracle" in Johannesburg on the weekend. According to the experts, Hinn and his colleagues made thousands of dollars disappear from the bank accounts of worshippers, before making the money reappear in offshore accounts.

Hinn's followers say there is nothing supernatural about the movement of funds from South African to American banks, but veteran observers of paranormal events are adamant that a verifiable miraculous event took place.

The miracle was widely publicized over the weekend by News24.com, which reported that Pastor Todd Koontz, one of Hinn's on-stage colleagues, told worshippers that God would turn them into millionaires or billionaires within twenty-four hours if they donated $1,000 by credit card.

According to News24.com, hundreds of worshippers mobbed the stage with their credit cards after Koontz told them that the window of opportunity for the blessing was only two minutes.

This morning investigators from the Vatican, as well as representatives of the scientific community, agreed that a miracle had taken place. "A fool and his money are easily parted, but this was something special," said head investigator, Cardinal Dante Purgatorio.

www.hayibo.com

Psychologist Gunter Glibb agreed.

"To make that many adults behave in such a profoundly silly manner, to hand over thousands in return for a 120-second shot at being written a cheque by some sort of imaginary heavenly cashier – something more than idiocy, ignorance, naivety and greed was at work here."

The South African organizers of the weekend's gathering could not be reached for comment on the alleged miracle, but hotel staff said that they had last been seen checking out in the early hours of Sunday morning, "giving each other high-fives and lighting cigars with smouldering R200 notes".

Meanwhile journalists at all of South Africa's major media stables are eagerly waiting to hear from any person who became a millionaire or billionaire twenty-four hours after making their donation to Hinn's Miracle Crusade.

According to a leading Johannesburg editor, three worshippers have come forward so far.

"The first two were a couple who got an email from the widow of a Nigerian prince, promising them $200 million if they sent a $500 administration fee," he said.

"Ag shame, they were pretty stoked, atnd they'd already sent the money, so we didn't say anything."

He said the third had been a Ms Frillypanties Mazakadza, who said she had been given $600 million at work the day after attending the Crusade.

However it was quickly established that this had been a tip at the Harare coffee shop where she works as a waitress.

search results related to: heavenly cashier

SA TO FIELD REPRESENTATIVE TEAMS, SPRINGBOKS CALL UP 8 WOMEN, 5 CHILDREN

PRETORIA. South African sports administrators have bowed to sustained pressure by the country's politicians and have agreed to field teams in future that accurately represent the demographics of the country. As part of the new deal, the Springboks will now feature 8 women, 5 children, and one pensioner, 6 of whom must be medically obese.

Since 1994 sporting codes have come under increasing pressure from lawmakers to be truly representative, and today's decision was hailed as a major step forward in South Africa's sporting fortunes.

"Why stop at race?" said Xolile Ntsebesa, chairman of Parliament's Joint Committee on Hard Sums. "If transformation is to be genuine and not just skin deep, we need to embrace all demographics in a real way."

According to the new legislation, all national teams will be required to field a representative from almost every lobby in the country. This means that 51 percent of all international caps must be women, 30 percent must be younger than 15, almost half must be morbidly obese, a quarter must speak Zulu, and half must have an IQ lower than 100.

Asked if the new legislation meant that 20 percent of all players would also have to be HIV-positive, Ntsebesa said that President Thabo Mbeki's internet research had proved that this figure was "wildly exaggerated", but conceded that between 5 and 10 percent of players would probably need to supplement their half-time oranges with African potatoes and garlic.

However, he denied that the new quota system was in denial about South African realities.

"On the contrary," said Ntsebesa, "we accept that 40 percent of South Africans are unemployed. This means that to be truly representative, six Springboks will have to remain technically unemployed, and will therefore not be paid."

He conceded, however, that these six would be allowed to raise funds for kit and tours by selling inflatable crocodiles at traffic lights and washing cars with muddy water.

www.hayibo.com

TEEN WHO CORRECTED NASA ASTEROID DATA HAS 1 IN 3.4 BILLION CHANCE OF FEELING UP GIRLS

ANC WORRIED "FOREIGN" MBEKI A PRIME TARGET FOR XENOPHOBIC ATTACK

BERLIN. Nico Marquardt, the German teen who this week embarrassed NASA scientists by proving that the odds on a deadly meteor impact were 1 in 450 and not 1 in 45000, has a 1 in 2 chance of having his underpants pulled over his head, while experts agree that he probably has a 1 in 3.4 billion chance of getting to feel under girls' bras.

Marquardt, 13, made international headlines this week with his claim that NASA had grossly miscalculated the odds of the asteroid Apophis striking Earth.

While the scientific community examines his figures, the unscientific community has joined the debate and has revealed that Marquardt faces a bleak future if he continues doing complex mathematics.

According to figures released by Dork Rescue, an organization that cares for lost or rejected highly intelligent social misfits, the odds of one of Marquardt's female classmates allowing him to feel her up have plunged.

"Before, the odds were probably around 1 in 50,000," said Dork Rescue counsellor Heinrich Blumenthal. "A long shot, but not impossible, given that boys like Nico tend to be moody, solitary and soft-spoken, which can be very mysterious and appealing to certain girls."

However, he said, Marquardt's chances of a torrid encounter behind the school's bicycle shed had probably plunged to 1 in 3.4 billion after his discovery, because "nobody likes a show-off, especially not a clever one".

He added that he was "100 percent certain" that Marquardt had already had his underpants pulled over his head by classmates, and that there was still a 1 in 2 chance of it happening again, with a "1 in 7 chance of the elastic snapping and the pants coming right off and being thrown out of the window by bigger boys."

But he urged Marquardt not to lose hope.

"If he's right, and that 1-in-450 long shot comes off, and Apophis is set to obliterate Earth in a few years, he can always try the old 'Do you want to die a virgin?' routine.

"People tend to drop their standards when faced with global apocalypse, so in this instance I'd say Nico would probably have a 1 in 500 shot at getting to third base." ✪

PRETORIA. The ruling African National Congress has explained that President Thabo Mbeki has not yet visited sites of xenophobic violence because security experts fear he might be targeted by angry mobs. Mbeki has spent a total of 19 days in South Africa since 2002, and according to a Presidency spokesperson most citizens now believe him to be a foreigner.

Mbeki has been severely criticised for failing to visit the sites worst hit by the xenophobic violence of the last two weeks, but according to Presidency spokesperson Spokes Mashabane, his absence has been a strategic decision.

"We must be pragmatic and concede that most of our citizens think that Mr Mbeki is a hybrid Shangaan-Belgian, dividing his time between the Rift Valley and The Hague.

"We are fully behind our President, but we also accept that if he shows his face in certain parts of Republic he will have a can of whupass opened on him."

He denied that Mbeki's television address to the nation on Sunday evening, in which the President called the violence a "disgrace", had been filmed four days ago on board the submarine SAS Sarafina 2.

"We categorically deny that the President is on a submarine in the South Atlantic.

"He is in fact on a corvette, the SAS Hansie Cronje, off the coast of Monte Carlo, where he has been engaging world leaders on issues such as global warming, roulette, and fly-fishing."

Meanwhile aide organisations and human rights lobbyists say they have been overwhelmed by the outpouring of support for dispossessed and homeless immigrants.

"We've given a fantastic amount of food, clothing and money to poor and hungry Zimbabweans and Mozambicans," said social worker Glenda Kemp.

"Maybe next year we might consider giving something to poor and hungry South Africans. "Maybe even throw in an extra few blankets if they learn to speak French with those sexy Congolese accents."

She added that this was "just a thought, and nothing to lose sleep over." ✪

www.hayibo.com

OFFICIAL: MUGABE AND MBEKI ARE HOTTEST NEW CELEBRITY COUPLE

PRETORIA. After months of speculation Robert Mugabe and Thabo Mbeki have confirmed that they are in fact an item, and have been seeing each other privately "for years".

Holding hands shyly in their first public appearance since Mugabe's attempt at rigging last month's general election, 'Mubeki' said they hoped the world would respect their wishes.

Asked what those wishes were, Mugabe said he hoped that "the whites and the gays" would stop trying to enforce "gay whiteness masquerading as democracy" on Zimbabwe's heterosexual black serfs.

Mbeki said he neither supported nor rejected Mugabe's views on whites and gays.

"It's not for me to say," he said, beaming proudly and looking radiant in a new black suit. "Robert is his own man. We love and respect each other. If he wants my opinion on an issue, he gives it to me.

"Otherwise my role in our relationship is to look good, and to wipe the spit off his glasses when the whites and the homosexuals make him angry, and to bring him his slippers before bedtime."

Asked what their plans for the future were, the celebrity couple said they were looking forward to some quality time on a game farm outside Harare.

"I'm going to sleep for ten hours a day with cucumbers on my eyes," giggled Mbeki, giving Mugabe's hand a squeeze. "Robert says he's got some errands in the main vote-counting station in town, but I don't pry."

And after that? Will there be a honeymoon for 'Mubeki'?

"A world cruise," said Mbeki. "We're going everywhere!"

"Except England," added Mugabe. "And the International Criminal Court in The Hague."

search results related to: african item

SURVEY

The mediation efforts in Zimbabwe have taught us that:

○ Elections are just a formality as long as you kill the right people

○ If you want to hold hands with a man in a rapidly homophobic continent, make sure you're both presidents

○ Life begins at 80 when you're an insane despot

○ Thabo Mbeki looks hot when he's cross

www.hayibo.com

BITTER AND DISILLUSIONED LIEWE HEKSIE PACKING FOR PERTH

BLOMMELAND. They call her Liewe Heksie but Lavinia is her name. She's the cleverest witch she knows, and she's even been to the moon. But for Liewe Heksie, 56, these words ring hollow.

"It sounded much better in Afrikaans," she says. "Now everything is in English or Xhosa." Middle-aged, bitter and disillusioned with the new South Africa, Heksie is emigrating to Australia.

Lavinia is the first to admit that the years have been unkind to her. The dirty blonde fringe is streaked with grey and the black velvet dress is pockmarked with cigarette burns.

"It's been a real struggle since they canned the show," she says, lighting one of the Lucky Strikes that have left her with severe emphysema.

"If I still had the show, flip, oke, I wouldn't be eating pilchards off a Tupperware lid now, genuine."

But, she says, the loss of stardom and wealth has paled into insignificance next to the loss of her dearest friends. Her eyes fill with tears as she recalls her beloved cat, Matewis.

"We put him to sleep in 1997," she says. "He got cancer in his brain and stomach, and on his nose, and in one ear, plus his tail went sort of vrot."

She blames the asbestos in the walls and ceiling of the council flat she's called home since her television show went off air in the late 1980s.

"It's also why Blommie doesn't come here any more," she adds. "He visited a few times in about 1991, but he said it was giving him migraines, and then he stopped coming."

She says she finally lost touch with her oldest friend after the elf announced his homosexuality in 1999.

"It still makes me very heartsore when I think about how we parted," she says, lighting another Lucky Strike.

"I'm not homophobic. It just came as a surprise. So when he said, 'Heksie, ek is 'n gay stoute kabouter!' I said 'Haai oe, Blommie, dis nie mooi nie'.

"He totally took it up the wrong way. Ag nee, wait, that also sounds homophobic. But you know what I mean."

She says she will always love Blommie, and hopes he can forgive her in time.

However, she believes Australia will provide fresh opportunities and a chance to start again.

"I still love South Africa, and it's great that we've got democracy now," she says. "Even if it did kill my show."

But, she adds, the advent of affirmative action has been a "bitter pill to sluk".

"I used to be the only good witch in the whole Gauteng-Blommeland region," she says.

"But after 1994 there were suddenly spell-quotas and magical Sotho snakes and tokkeloshes and fokken Liewe Swart Heksies wherever you looked.

"Skuus dat ek so vloek," she adds hastily. She is also quick to insist that she is not a racist, adding that she enjoyed working with many black actors such as Karel Kraai on 'Wielie Walie'.

She dusts off a yellowing photograph of her with Matewis and carefully packs it into her small suitcase, before heading for the door for the last time.

"I think South Africa is a wonderful country with a great future," she says.

"Just not for white 56-year-old Afrikaans-speaking practitioners of the occult."

search results related to: liewe heksie

STEVE HOFMEYR PERFORATES COLON, AFRIKAANS ROCKERS EXAMINE OWN SPHINCTERS

PRETORIA. Afrikaans pop stars are reportedly flocking to emergency rooms around the country in the hope of finding something wrong with their rectums. Steve Hofmeyr's emergency surgery this week for a perforated colon has triggered a wave of goodwill and publicity, and many stars apparently hope a similar ordeal will boost their own careers.

According to emergency room staff, the last 24 hours have seen a dramatic increase in the number of Afrikaans pop singers asking for doctors to examine their rectums.

"On an average night we get maybe one or two," said nurse Phumzile Zondo at Pretoria's Erwin Rommel Memorial Hospital. "But today it's been crazy. Just puffer jackets, platform takkies and blond highlights wherever you look."

She said she had seen Kurt Darren in the emergency ward, looking "thin and frightened, which was sad because normally he looks chubby and brave", but could not confirm reports that he had been discussing the possibility of having some sort of dramatic procedure inflicted on his sphincter that might boost album sales and get him a four-page spread of 'pragfotos' and 'skokfotos' in Huisgenoot.

Staff at Cape Town's Groote Schuur Hospital said that Dozi had checked himself in for an examination yesterday evening, but added that it was for severely traumatized scalp follicles and not for anything rectal. According to nurses, Dozi had not yet heard of Hofmeyr's colon, as he had been out all day riding a horse and yodelling.

There were no reports of any Afrikaans singers of any kind, whether rock, pop, folk or country, checking into the Chris Hani Baragwanath Hospital in Soweto, although several witnesses claim to have seen Koos Kombuis sitting anxiously in a car outside, chewing his nails, before driving off again.

Meanwhile Hofmeyr, who has sold over 3.6 billion albums in the Free State alone, without the help of a perforated colon, is reportedly recovering well after his frightening ordeal.

"Steve is a fighter," said surgeon Dr Hannes Malan. "He doesn't only have a big voice. He's got a big heart too.

"I don't know if the old school of Afrikaans pop would have bounced back this hard. If Bles or Gé or even Andre Schwartz had pulled a poepstring, we might have had a much more tragic outcome." ★

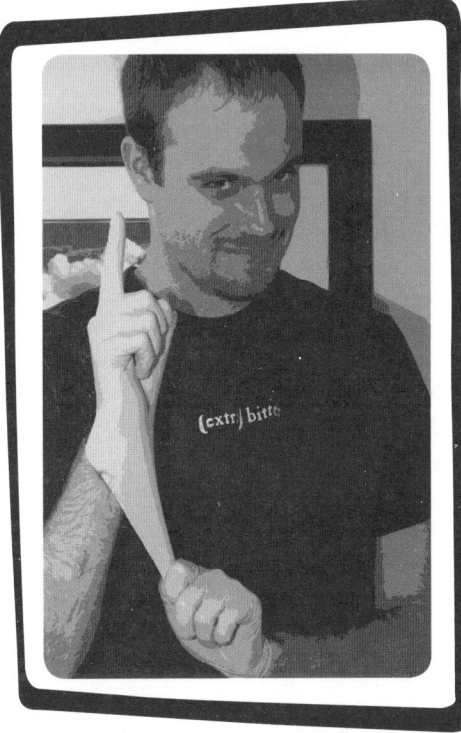

search results related to: colon examination

OTHER BREAKING NEWS

★ **Zimbabwe to cure cholera epidemic with Salma Hayek breast milk**

★ **Watson denies planning sex tape to bolster flagging image**

★ **Flatulent and senile, A-Team finally arrested after 36 years**

www.hayibo.com

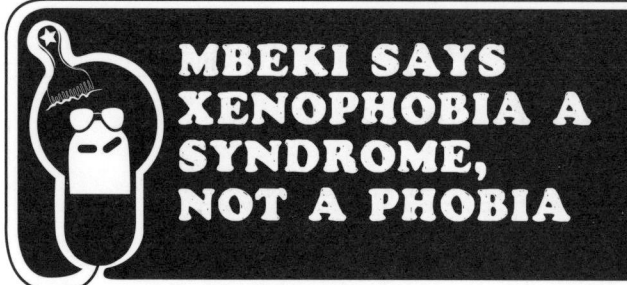

MBEKI SAYS XENOPHOBIA A SYNDROME, NOT A PHOBIA

JOHANNESBURG. As a wave of anti-immigrant violence sweeps through Johannesburg's townships, President Thabo Mbeki has warned his critics not to exaggerate the crisis. Speaking to the media this morning, Mbeki said that xenophobia was a syndrome and not a genuine phobia. He added that he has never personally known anyone with xenophobia.

Over 22 people have been killed in the escalating violence, with mobs of South Africans apparently trying to purge foreigners from the townships around Johannesburg. However, Mbeki told the press not to jump to conclusions.

Citing "exhaustive research done on the Internet last night", Mbeki explained that the word 'xenophobia' was wildly inaccurate and was leading to a misdiagnosis of the current violence.

"We need to be less eager to believe in this thing called xenophobia," he said. "Arachnophobia, yes. Spiders are horrible. But what is a xeno? There is no such thing."

However, he added that the word was most commonly used in an African context.

"This makes me wonder whether in fact 'xeno' isn't perhaps some sort of racist codeword for an African," he said. "I ask you. Just because there is an X in front of a word, does that make it automatically African?"

Mbeki was also quick to reassure the international community, specifically world football governing body FIFA.

"I want to tell all those players, administrators and fans who are coming here in 2010, please do not worry.

"By all accounts the violence is being fuelled by criminal elements, and by the belief that foreigners are stealing our jobs and our women."

He said that as long as international visitors stayed away from criminals and did not ask out local girls or set up discount spaza shops in townships, they were "unlikely to be set on fire".

Opposition parties have been calling on Mbeki to enforce law and order by sending the South African National Defence Force into the townships, but Mbeki dismissed this out of hand.

"This is not an acceptable solution. The SANDF has spent the last ten years training for African peacekeeping missions. Our soldiers are totally focused on only one thing, and that is shooting at small groups of Burundians and so forth who are running away with their possessions on their heads.

"There would be a bloodbath, and FIFA have insisted that we keep bloodbaths to a minimum before 2010."

However, he said that his government was setting up a task team whose role would be to "ask difficult questions".

"For example, if you set a Zimbabwean on fire and there's no-one from FIFA around to see it, did it really happen? And more importantly, if it did happen, how is it my problem?"

SA SUBMARINE BREAKS DEPTH RECORD AFTER ACCIDENTAL SINKING

CAPE TOWN. One of South Africa's controversial new submarines, the SS Constitution, has broken the record for the deepest dive after its novice crew accidentally sank the vessel and wedged it into a seabed canyon in the South Atlantic. The navy has confirmed that the crew are "elated and will savour the achievement until the batteries and tinned food run out".

The submarine was named after the South African constitution earlier this year, after the navy asked the ANC's National Executive Committee to "suggest names that might represent something in South Africa's recent history that has disappeared without a ripple".

Rear Admiral Nelson Chikane said the NEC's suggestions had included Scorpion, Zanele Mbeki and Amor Vittone, but that ultimately government and the navy had felt that Constitution was the most appropriate name as, like its namesake, "it could always be changed later".

Briefing journalists at the Simonstown naval base this morning, Chikane said that the record had been broken after some of the cadets had opened the hatch "to get some air" at a depth of 500 metres.

www.hayibo.com

He added that subsequent efforts to save the vessel had resulted in "agitated behaviour" from the novice crew, including "accidentally locking the captain in the fridge, firing the instruction manual out of a torpedo tube, and putting the submarine into second gear when reverse was required".

However, he said that the navy was proud of how the seamen had turned a crisis into a triumph.

"Approximately three hours after the accident, the Constitution reached a depth of 2,100 metres whereupon it wedged safely inside a narrow canyon, upside down and tilting slightly towards the stern."

He confirmed that this was 2,100 metres deeper than any of the Navy's current submarines had dived, and said that the office of President Thabo Mbeki had already radioed the submariners, congratulating them for "reaching new depths just when it seemed that South Africans couldn't sink any lower".

Meanwhile Deputy Minister of Defence Caligula Mshenge has reassured panicked family members, saying that a rescue operation is being planned.

"As soon as we train another crew, and find the immobiliser clicker for the SS Queen Modjadji, we're on our way," he told a media briefing in Pretoria.

"We will bring them home. This I vow."

Mshenge declined to elaborate further on his vow or on the condition in which the submariners would be brought home, but he promised that if rescuers discovered that "things had got a bit soggy" aboard the Constitution, the families of the submariners would be compensated with a gift pack of ANC T-shirts and caps, and lifetime free passes to uShaka Marine World in Durban "to give them the sense of being close to their loved ones." ✪

search results related to: sinking submarine

CRIME SYNDICATES COMPLAIN PROPOSED ANTI-CRIME MARCH MAKES IT TOO EASY

JOHANNESBURG. Two of Joburg's largest crime syndicates have warned that the so-called Million Man March Against Crime, scheduled for June 10, has been badly planned and "will all end in tears". According to the syndicates, the march is likely to leave at least 250,000 homes unattended, with that number rising to 500,000 if women are permitted to join the protest.

Speaking on condition of anonymity at a bed-and-breakfast in Fourways, a spokesman for the syndicates said that in-house market research had confirmed that Johannesburg's suburbs would be "pretty much one gigantic sitting duck on June 10".

"It's not rocket science," he told journalists. "If a million men are marching against crime, and if just a quarter of them live in some sort of formal habitation, that's 250,000 empty homes."

It is currently unclear whether or not women will be permitted to join the Million Man March Against Crime, but the spokesman said his employers were "hoping for the best".

"We're assuming the honeys will be marching too," he said. "I mean, damn, it's not called the Million Man March for Misogyny Against Bitchez, even if the name is a little iffish in gender terms."

However, he denied that Johannesburg's criminals were looking forward to the march, saying that top crimelords had been disappointed by the naiveté of the concept, and that it had left them feeling "betrayed and disillusioned".

"We take a lot of pride in our work," he said. "It's taken dedication, perseverance, and massive amounts of tik to get where we are today. But more than that, it's taken courage.

"You need serious guts to invade one of these northern suburbs houses nowadays, with the kind of firepower they're packing."

"To just have it all handed to you like this ... It really makes you wonder why you bother. They might as well just switch off the lawn lasers and give the Rottweiler a rohypnol before they leave.

"If we wanted to rob people without any chance of being prosecuted, without breaking a sweat, and all while being amateurishly obvious about it, we would have become Members of Parliament." ✪

www.hayibo.com

ZUMA CAMP CALLS FOR DISCIPLINE UNTIL 2010, ALL BETS OFF AFTER THAT

PIETERMARITZBURG. Jacob Zuma's camp has asked his militant supporters to show restraint until after the 2010 World Cup so as not to endanger the staging of the event. However, once the event was over, said a spokesman, "cadres should feel free to uphold democracy in whatever manner they choose, using whichever projectiles and flammables come to hand."

Observers say this is the first time the Zuma camp has made any effort to curb the confrontational rhetoric of the Mkhonto weSizwe veterans and ANC Youth League members who have vowed to plunge the country into chaos if Zuma is found guilty of corruption, or if he is given his day in court, or not, or something, just because.

The reading of the statement was delayed briefly while paramedics treated an elderly woman whose wooden replica AK-47 had become entangled in her leopard-skin bra, leaving her with severe splinter-related injuries.

According to the statement, it was essential for Zuma's supporters not to do anything that could jeopardize the pension plans of either Zuma or the National Executive Committee.

"Cadres must understand that the 2010 World Cup is going to make the party and a number of senior comrades extremely rich, and when senior comrades are rich, democracy is rich," read the statement.

"We therefore call upon them to behave in a way that goes against their more incendiary democratic urges, and to refrain from performing acts of love for Msholozi that involve threats to kill, eliminate, remove or otherwise terminally inconvenience political opponents."

It went on to state that FIFA and European policy-makers were not familiar with South African democratic traditions.

"What we call rolling mass action, they call mob justice. What we call lobbying, they call intimidation. What we call the fruits of liberation, they call a bribe."

It said that these were "ugly Eurocentric terms", but that they would have to be tolerated for the time being.

Meanwhile Zuma's camp has confirmed that it is working on a contingency plan to deal with possible fallout if the World Cup is withdrawn from South Africa at the eleventh hour.

Dubbed 'Operation Jump Up and Down', the plan involves "burning some railway carriages, emptying municipal rubbish bins onto pavements, and breaking down the symbols of capitalist greed, such as shop windows and display cabinets of electronics goods stores, cellphone vendors, and branches of American Swiss".

search results related to: camp zuma

OTHER BREAKING NEWS

★ SACP happy to retain power without contesting election

★ Last honest public official to auction integrity to highest bidder

★ Somali pirates started reign of terror with mixed tapes at home

www.hayibo.com

RAMPAGE SCHOOLBOYS TO BE PUNISHED WITH BLACKS, NORMAL SIZED GIRLS

CAPE TOWN. An elite Cape Town private school has confirmed that the Matric class that ran amok last week will be punished by making them talk to a black person and appear in public with either a Jew or a Muslim. The schoolboys have been granted a farewell dance but they will not be allowed to take anorexic blonde partners as has been the case since 1903.

The school, which has asked Hayibo.com not to name it as its pupils and staff face enough ridicule on a day-to-day basis for having underdeveloped chins, made headlines last week after its senior class ran through the school damaging property and leaving behind lewd graffiti.

According to an unnamed source, the violence had included "sexual abuse of a statue of Cecil John Rhodes in the Empire Memorial Quad, and the theft from the Chapel of a ceremonial dominatrix paddle used by headmasters since 1877".

This morning the current headmaster, who has been at the school since he was a foetus, said that the perpetrators would be harshly dealt with.

"I have instructed Matron to tell Mumsy to communicate it to Crispin the school factotum to tell the boys that we will not tolerate this kind of violence," said the headmaster.

"Unless of course it is standard homoerotic bullying sanctioned by the school's governing body, which this wasn't," he added.

He said that the punishment, to be meted out immediately, was intended to give the boys "a taste of real life beyond the ivy-covered walls of our Mother School" and would require them to "approach and speak to, for a period not exceeding half an hour, a genuine black person of African extraction, as well as appearing in a public space with a person of either Hebrew or Mohammedan extraction".

However, he said, the most severe punishment would involve the Matric farewell dance.

He explained that anorexic bottle-blonde women were the norm in the school's community, "understandably, as they are really the only things worth breeding with".

However, he said that this year the boys would be barred from bringing their regular partners to the dance, and would be required to bring girls who were "disturbingly normal, both in body shape and hair colour".

He said that the boys had been nauseated to learn that most women didn't have knee-bones that were wider than their thighs and didn't have shoulder blades that protruded enough to sever bra straps.

He added that some of the boys, "the clever, poor ones who are here on scholarships", had encountered "fat brunettes" before, and were often related to them, but he said that the rest of the boys were "severely shocked". However, he said the school was beyond sympathy.

Meanwhile the reaction from the boys' girlfriends has been one of outrage and despair.

Tammy Rommel-Hess, 18, of Berchtesgaden Golf Estate in Bishopscourt, said that she and many of her friends had been working on their eating disorders for years, and that it would now all be a waste of countless hours spent hunched over the toilet.

"It was all part of a complex plan," she sobbed.

"Go to the Matric Dance, get married, have a son, and a back-up daughter in case the son needs an organ transplant, do modelling, run an art gallery in a mall, and finally emigrate to London."

Now, she said, her "dream was in tatters."

OTHER BREAKING NEWS

★ **Bursting property bubble causes glut of soccer moms**

★ **Parliament says Cape Town road closures reflect democracy**

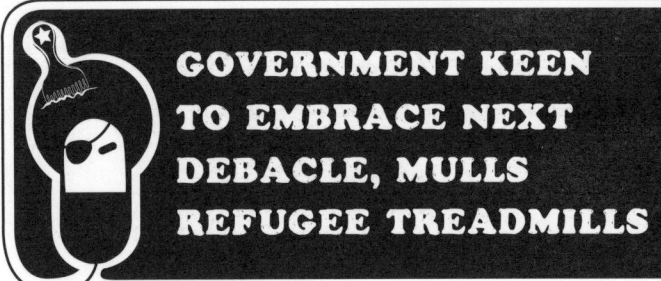

GOVERNMENT KEEN TO EMBRACE NEXT DEBACLE, MULLS REFUGEE TREADMILLS

PRETORIA. The South African government has rejected a warning by the United Nations that creating refugee camps would be a mistake. "Just because something is a mistake, is that a reason not to try?" said a spokesman at Luthuli House. "This government has a long and proud history of going ahead with plans that were clearly mistakes, and has it cost us votes? No."

According to spokesman Beowulf Ngema, the ANC and its voters had never shied away from potential catastrophes "just because some so-called expert says it's going to end in disaster".

"Our government has established an almost unrivalled legacy for embracing unpopular policies, whether we are talking about the so-called Aids malnutrition syndrome that has killed so many dozens of our people, or our efforts to ease the transition between Robert Mugabe's seventh and eighth terms in office.

"And our voters have stood by us all the way."

He said he believed that the ANC's electorate had also embraced the party's approach to potentially disastrous long-term projects.

"In every election since 1994 our numbers have swelled. This is because the masses have embraced our modern political ubuntu, which roughly translated means 'I am possibly making a big mistake because you are possibly making a big mistake, but if we both make a big mistake we can blame the Democratic Alliance and Buthelezi.'

"Our voters are not fools. They know that continuing to give us power without accountability is a mistake, that we're just in it for the money and will almost certainly screw them over as soon as we've secured our pensions; but they are willing to be stakeholders in our risk-taking vision."

He also urged South Africans to "look on the bright side" of the crisis, saying that refugee camps might provide the country with a solution to its electricity shortage.

"The generating potential of 50,000 refugees running like mad on treadmills is immense," said Ngema. "And it's not like they've got anything else to do, you know?

"If they slow down, you deport them. If they produce more power than you need, you export it to Zimbabwe, where it is transmitted via police electrodes directly into the genitalia of MDC supporters."

He said more power adhering to MDC genitalia would translate into more refugees, which in turn would result in more people on treadmills.

"It's what we call renewable energy," he said. ★

PRESIDENT OF NIGERIA BEATEN UP TO GIVE HIM TASTE OF LIFE IN SA

CAPE TOWN. Official xenophobes have beaten Nigerian President Umaru Yar'Adua to a bloody pulp on the second day of his first state visit to South Africa. Presidency protocol experts said that the beating was intended to give Yar'Adua an authentic taste of life in South Africa, and to let him more closely understand the plight of victims of xenophobia.

According to Gladiola Xorile, the Presidency's Head of Protocol, the experience was carefully planned and adhered to the strictest international standards.

"Most Africans who have been attacked in the past weeks were attacked by their neighbours, when they least expected it," she said, explaining why Yar'Adua had been assaulted by seven waiters as he sat down to a state banquet.

She said the officially appointed goons had "thrown the kitchen sink at him", but conceded that the kitchen sink had not been as effective a missile as they had hoped.

"It was very difficult to aim, with all the taps and everything," she said, adding that it had veered off target before ricocheting off Nkosazana Dlamini-Zuma's head-dress.

Fortunately, she said, there were "old Zanu classics" to fall back on, such as cricket bats, coal-scuttles and cutlery, which were "applied to his sensitive bits for about three hours."

However, she vehemently denied that the evening had ended with the South African contingent stealing the Nigerian Presidential jet.

www.hayibo.com

"We considered adhering to the full xenophobic programme, which would have required us to beat him up, steal his jet, and then set fire to his home, but we realised that this would require us to set fire to most of Nigeria, which would have had legal repercussions."

"Besides, our President already has a jet, and if we need another one, well, that's what tax-payers are for."

Asked if Robert Mugabe would receive the same treatment if he visited the country, Xorile said that "plans, accessories and a variety of body oils were in place" for such an eventuality.

"Nobody can accuse us of favouritism," she said, adding that if Mugabe set foot in South Africa, President Mbeki would "probably personally smack his bare bottom with a moulded latex feather-duster". ✪

search results related to: kitchen sink

SURVEY

The best thing to do with your money at the moment is to:

○ Invest in growth industries like narcotics, war and house repossession

○ Give it all to Hayibo.com. You are growing sleepy. Give it all you Hayibo.com. You are feeling heavy... Give it all to Hayibo.com...

○ Give it all to the poor and remind them of that when the revolution starts

○ Get your facelift now because you won't be able to afford it when you're old

SANDTON MAGAZINE HAILED AS JUST WHAT RICH WHITES NEED

JOHANNESBURG. The residents of Sandton have hailed the launch of lifestyle magazine 'Sandton', saying it will boost morale in a suburb long dogged by ennui, affluenza, and a non-specific loathing for the poor. The cover of the first issue features two wealthy young white people "to help frightened Sandtonians forget about Alexandra township next door".

The magazine's tagline is 'The good life in the great north', but the magazine's lavish launch last night was briefly interrupted by a fracas, when four Mozambicans wandered into the ballroom apparently in search of the good life in the great north, and had to be tazered before being shipped to a refugee internment camp.

According to publisher Adolph Oppenheimer, Sandton's editorial policy is built around using the word 'Africa' as often as is realistically possible.

"We felt it was important to foreground Africa in the magazine," he said, "because if you keep saying it enough people might not notice that we're glorifying an obscene temple to conspicuous consumption on the planet's poorest continent."

While the first issue is largely about branding, styling, and why lip gloss is more important than reading a book, future issues promise more in-depth features.

Oppenheimer said his team was already researching articles such as 'The Blacks: can we live without them?', 'Ten Zuma-proof offshore investments you can hide from the taxman' and 'Botox your Botox: why your face can never be paralyzed enough'.

He said there would also be strong reader interactivity, with a team of experts dedicated to answering readers' questions.

"A lot of people in Sandton want to know: are Malawians more trustworthy than Xhosas, or should you get a Zulu garden boy?

"Likewise, should we be looking at Perth or London post-2010?"

However, he said, the magazine would ultimately send out a positive message.

"We want to remind people that there is no problem this country can throw at you that you can't solve with electric fencing and a pedicure." ✪

www.hayibo.com

MUGABE WANTS TIME OUT FROM BEING EVIL BASTARD TO FOCUS ON INSANITY

ROME. Robert Mugabe says he would like to use his autumn years to take some time away from being an evil bastard, and focus on "simply being gloriously insane". Mugabe, who is currently in Rome in defiance of an international travel ban, also thanked the European Union for being "a bunch of gutless pussies who can't even stand by their own resolutions".

Speaking to journalists while partner Thabo Mbeki gave him a foot-massage, Mugabe said that he had tired of being an evil bastard, and that he wanted a chance to fully embrace his insanity before he got too old to enjoy it.

"Being an evil bastard limits you in so many ways," he said. "For instance, sometimes you just want to cuddle a puppy. But the nation expects evil, and so you have to put the puppy in a calabash full of battery acid.

"However, being insane allows one a much wider range of responses. I can cuddle the puppy if I want, or put it in acid, or throw it at Thabo, or shoot it out of a cannon, or make it Minister of Finance.

"Each new day is a wonderful adventure when you're gloriously, completely, unashamedly insane."

However, Mugabe said he did not want to be too disparaging about being evil, as it had left him with many of his happiest memories.

"There have been a lot of evil bonbons over the years," he said, "and obviously I treasure those rigged elections as two of the highlights of my evil career."

But, he said, evil was a younger man's game, and it was time to move on.

"There's a lot I'd like to accomplish, now that I'm completely insane," he said. "For instance, I'd still like to hawk a loogie across the Security Council table into Ban Ki-moon's eye."

He said he was also taking ukulele lessons, was learning to breakdance, and was working on a recipe for exploding poisonous muffins.

"The muffins will be my insane magnum opus," he said. "I'm going to shave off all my body hair, get Thabo to cover me in cooking fat, put clothes-pegs on my nipples, slip into my stilettos, and then force-feed the muffins to Tony Blair.

"When he explodes I'm going to sing 'Macho Man' by the Village People, and then probably have a nap."

Thabo Mbeki was hesitant to comment, but admitted that these revelations were new to him and that he was "a little creeped out".

search results related to: macho man mugabe

Sagittarius

Sagittarius Nov 22 - Dec 21

A late-night drinking game involving a bottle of Captain Morgan and a tube of KY gel will end in the emergency room, with a doctor confirming that you've got a little Captain in you.

www.hayibo.com

COSAS DEFENDS ZUMA MARCH, CALLS FOR VOTING AGE TO BE LOWERED TO 7

JOHANNESBURG. The Congress of South African Students has defended last week's action in which it forced schoolchildren to leave their classes and march in support of Jacob Zuma, saying that education was no longer a necessity in South Africa. "Many of us don't have a secondary education," said a Cosas spokesman, "and it hasn't hurt our chances of getting high-paying jobs in Government."

Hundreds of schoolchildren were rounded up by Cosas in township schools around Johannesburg and taken by bus and train to the city centre where they protested Zuma's innocence by sucking lollipops, braiding each other's hair, and writing inspirational messages about Beyonce Knowles in TipEx on their blazers.

Spokesman Facebrick Ndlovu dismissed criticisms that the march should have taken place on a Saturday instead of a school day, and also that Cosas was squandering taxpayers' money.

"I have personally been told by many of our child cadres that they felt the march was a success largely because it happened on a school day," he said.

"In fact they have demanded that Cosas stage a similar march every Friday, and perhaps some Thursdays as well, in order to fully enflame their patriotic zeal."

He added that the pupils had also asked for "donuts, maybe a DJ, and a jumping castle, also to increase their awareness of the injustice facing Comrade Zuma".

"As for the issue of the funds we used, we will not apologize. The people who pay tax are mostly those who have passed Matric, and clearly this is not our demographic.

"Nobody even vaguely connected with Cosas has passed Matric, or come close on a second or third attempt, and we are determined to uphold those traditions in the coming years."

He conceded that most of the children had not known why they had left their schools or what the march was about, but he denied that disrupting their exam preparation was helping to produce a generation of uncritical voting fodder.

"Even if I knew what a fodder was, I would deny this," said Ndlovu.

"We are simply helping nurture and develop new skills that are in desperately short supply in this country."

He said that these skills included "voting for Msholozi and writing protest manifestos in TipEx on the doors of public toilets".

Meanwhile Cosas has called on the government to lower the voting age to 7.

National chairperson Einstein Sodwana said that children needed to "have the burden of education lifted from them so that they can be free to fully engage in the revolution".

"If our Grade Ones can vote, why expend resources on controversial and damaging activities like teaching them how to read or do sums?

"In our view we need a much more nurturing education system for our little ones, whereby all they do at school is Show and Tell.

"We show them a picture of Msholozi, and tell them to vote for him."

search results related to: zuma and kids

www.hayibo.com

EMBOLDENED LEKOTA TO ADD MORE VOWELS TO NAME

PRETORIA. Rebel politician Mosiuoa Lekota says he will reward loyalty at the polls by adding more vowels to his name because the masses like a chief with a long name. According to Lekota aides, he is likely to rename himself Moiiuoaieiosiouaeuuoia Lekota, although pundits agree it will make little difference as his name will still be unpronounceable.

Lekota and former Gauteng premier Mbhazima Barney Barnato Shilowa are currently planning their first national conference, where they will try to explain to voters why their policies are completely different from and entirely identical to those of the ANC.

"People are still a bit confused," said Lekota spokesman Pipsqueak Sephuma.

"They are saying, 'But aren't you the same politicians who got the country into a mess under Thabo Mbeki, and endorsed quiet diplomacy with Mugabe, and denied Aids, and bought weapons while your people starved, and undermined the judiciary, and damaged race relations, and ignored crime?'

"But what we're saying is…"

"What we're saying is…"

He then asked to be excused, saying he had "made a terrible terrible mistake".

He is believed to have resigned.

However, new party organizers say they are confident that their new slogan – "Better the Corrupt and Arrogant Politicians You Know than the Corrupt and Arrogant Politicians You Don't" – will make a difference at the polls next year.

And Lekota has vowed to "give back to the people" by dramatically lengthening his name should the party make serious inroads in Parliament.

According to one party insider who did not wish to be named but is believed to be Lekota's auntie Ivy, the politician has "always understood that the masses like chiefs with a long name".

"If you can't have a big mshini then you must have a big name," she said, adding that Lekota had always had "something of a crush on Sri Lankan cricketers because they have those wonderful long names."

She revealed that Lekota's imaginary friend as a child had been called Nelson Terrorpatrickterrorpatrick Lekotalekotalekota Youdaman Lekota.

"That's why he got on so well with Thabo Mbeki," she said. "Thabo also had an imaginary friend. Two, actually. Funny little pixies, one on each shoulder, and they'd tell him what to do and what to say, and he grew to love them very much."

Asked what their names had been, she said she thought they might have been called Essop and Aziz Pahad.

search results related to: mosiuoa lekota

HOROSCOPE

Taurus Apr 20 - May 20

Do not under any circumstances trust your horoscope this week.

DA ELECTION OBSERVER OUTRAGED BY SHORTAGE OF TONIC WATER IN ZIMBABWE

JOHANNESBURG. A visibly distressed Gwyneth D'Arcy, the Democratic Alliance's spokeswoman for Native Affairs, has described scenes of shocking neglect in Zimbabwe after returning with a group of South African election observers. "I saw members at the Victoria Gymkhana Club queuing for tonic water," she said. "And there's no ice."

Speaking to reporters at the party's Gauteng compound under the Dainfern golf estate, D'Arcy said she had been "sickened" by what she had been forced to witness in Zimbabwe.

"Do you know that the children don't wear pants?" she said. "You can see the little boys' willies and everything. "And there are dogs everywhere, beautiful Rhodesian ridgebacks, just wandering around without breeding papers or microchips."

She said there was clearly an urgent need to restore some sort of order in the troubled African state.

"I would suggest microchips for the children, and obviously pants, and then some sort of breeding papers."
D'Arcy said Zimbabweans were "still the wonderful, smiling, chipper and obedient fellows" she remembered from her girlhood on the Lee-Enfield 303 cotton plantation, but that they were suffering brutal deprivations.

"I think I shall never forget the sight of people – white people, mind – queuing at the bar of the Victoria Gymkhana Club and being rationed to three cans of Schweppes tonic and two shots of gin each, per hour, six days a week."

She also appealed to South Africans to "open their hearts and their golf bags" to Zimbabwe's dispossessed. "Everything helps," she said. "Cashmere sweaters, putters, anything."

OBAMA '08: ANC MPS QUIT POSTS TO JOIN OBAMA

PRETORIA. Leading ANC politicians have ended speculation about their future, announcing that they will travel to the US to seek senior positions in Barack Obama's new cabinet. The rebel politicians said they had delayed their decision until a clear and powerful winner had emerged, adding that Obama was now somewhat more powerful than Jacob Zuma.

Addressing the media at OR Tambo International Airport this morning, a spokesman for the contingent of ANC politicians said that Obama's win had put the current power struggle in South Africa in perspective.

"Every South Africa politician understands that the first duty of a public servant is to serve his own financial interests," said spokesman Mandrax Phiri.

"We are 100 percent loyal to Comrade Jacob Zuma, but he will understand that we are also 110 percent loyal to our pensions."

He said that ultimately firepower had also been a consideration.

"Every true patriot knows that wonderful anthem 'Awlethu' Mshini Wam'," said Phiri.

"But the reality is that in January Mr Obama will be given the launch codes, and you can't really compare 'Awlethu' Mshini Wam' with 'Awlethu' Nuclear Warheads Wam'."

He conceded that the ANC faction was taking a risk in buying one-way tickets to Washington, but said he was confident that they had the skills to secure high-paying consulting jobs in the Obama administration.

"This is Obama's honeymoon period," said Phiri. "He can do no wrong.

"But that will change. He'll get corrupt, and he'll lie, and he'll backtrack, and he'll deny.

"And when he does he'll need experienced people who have spent years deflecting criticism, denying wrongdoing, covering up corruption, and accusing critics of being racists. E voila!

"It's a licence to print money. Amandla Obama! Viva Green Card Viva!"

search results related to: tonic water

www.hayibo.com

GAUTRAIN CONSTRUCTION DEVASTATING GAUTENG GUMMI BEAR COMMUNITIES

JOHANNESBURG. They're dashing and daring, courageous and caring, faithful and friendly with stories to share, but hundreds of Gummi bears have already been pulped by tunnelling machinery under Johannesburg. According to conservationists, the Gautrain will wipe out Gauteng's population of the magical bouncing bears "far more quickly than Duke Igthorn could ever have imagined".

Construction workers on various Gautrain tunneling sites say they are finding fewer and fewer traces of the magical bears.

"It used to be that we'd see them once every couple of weeks," said mechanic Josiah Mphundu.

"We'd break through some rock, and we would see these bears, bouncing here and there and everywhere.

"But not any more."

Crews operating the massive tunnel-boring drill confirmed that they were having to stop work more frequently to scrape the remains of Gummi bears off the specialized drill-head.

"It's sad, but what are you going to do?" asked borer driver Blakkie Swart. "When I was a kid you'd hear them, all through the forest, singing out in chorus, marching along as their song filled the air.

"But now you sort of hear like a small scream, and then a kind of a wet noise, like someone smashing a watermelon with a hammer, and then you have to stop and scrape all that yellow and blue fur off the drillhead.

"It's kak depressing."

Conservationist Eric Monkey-Chandler said that efforts to save the remaining bears had been hampered by a lack of knowledge about the secretive animals.

"Magic and mystery are part of their history," he said.

He said that the bears once inhabited the forests of Mpumalanga before the apartheid homeland system forced them to the cities, where they went underground.

"It destroyed their whole culture. They stopped producing Gummiberry juice in the late 1970s, and they've been drinking mostly meths since then."

He said it had been "heartbreaking" to watch the decline of the species.

"Once, when the legend was growing, they took pride in knowing that they fought for what's right in whatever they did.

"But it's hard to fight for what's right when you're stoned on meths."

He said any survivors in Gauteng would probably be transported to the Western Cape, where a handful of Gummi bear communities still survive, working on wine estates as grapepressers.

He added that he and his colleagues would be monitoring the Western Cape's bears closely, after receiving reports of exploitation and the use of the 'dop' system.

"They give the bears a dop of Gummiberry juice, and then put a lid over the grape-pressing tank, so it's a hell of a noisy, violent situation down there."

However, he conceded, "tramping on grapes and being paid in the Gummi bear version of crack" was better than being "turned to pink mist" by tunnelling equipment. ★

search results related to: pulped gummi bears

MANDELA GIVEN OXYGEN AFTER TRYING TO BLOW OUT 90 TRICK CANDLES

QUNU. Nelson Mandela has been forced to have what aides are calling "a little lie-down with a bottle of oxygen" after trying unsuccessfully to blow out 90 trick candles on a birthday cake. The cake and candles were supplied by an embarrassed Essop and Aziz Pahad, who had hoped the candles would "symbolize the fire of freedom which can never be extinguished".

The Pahads later admitted that they "probably hadn't thought the whole thing through".

Celebrations in Qunu came to a halt when Mandela slowly slid out of his chair and under the table after trying to blow out the candles for fifteen minutes.

"Tata Madiba has the constitution of an ox," said an unnamed aide, "but seriously, who gives a 90-year-old trick candles? Seriously."

Mandela's disappearance under the table was not immediately noticed, as dessert had just been served and most guests were absorbed by their tiramisu. However, according to witnesses, Graca Machel realised something was amiss when she tried to feed her partner a spoonful of the pudding and found him gone.

Paramedics on the scene said that Mandela had not been in any danger or discomfort, and that he had "just gone beddy-bye for a few seconds".

"But seriously," added paramedic Needles Ngwenya, "who gives a 90-year-old trick candles? Seriously."

A spokesman for the Pahads said that the candles had been meant to "symbolize the fire of freedom which can never be extinguished".

"Plus everybody loves trick candles, with all the blowing, and then it's like 'Whoa!' when they re-light, and then everyone's like 'You've got a girlfriend!' or 'You can't blow out your candles!' and then you're like 'Geez, why can't I blow this out?' and then everyone is like, 'Check it, check it, you've got three girlfriends now!' and, and – yeah, when you put it like that, it probably wasn't appropriate."

Paramedic Ngwenya said that after ten minutes with an oxygen bottle Mandela was back on his feet and agitated about missing out on tiramisu.

"He got quite forceful when I told them there was only about a third of a bowl left," said Ngwenya.

"He said he didn't spend 27 years in prison to dip out on the sweets, and that there was going to be some arse-kicking if those damned cousins from East London had gone and jumped in the trough with their Tupperwares like they always do."

Mandela was given an ovation when he returned to the party, but had to ask the Pahads to refrain from kissing his feet, as he feared he might trip, and also found it "deeply creepy".

The Pahads later led a cheer of "Here's to the next 90 for Tata Madiba!", a gesture appreciated by the elder statesman, although he responded by suggesting that it was "unlikely" he would see his 180th birthday.

He said it was a "very sweet thing to say", but added that "sycophancy is all fun and games until someone tries to blow out trick candles and passes out."

"And who gives a 90-year-old trick candles?" he asked. "Seriously."

search results related to: mandela birthday cake

www.hayibo.com

AMERICANS CLAIM VICTORY IN 'OPERATION ROOSEVELT SE MA SE P**S'

CAPE TOWN. Cape Town's infamous Americans gang says the departure from Table Bay of the US aircraft-carrier USS Theodore Roosevelt was a "cowardly retreat by a gang of rival wannabe Americans", and has reclaimed the bay as Americans territory. According to a gang spokesman, the US warship retreated after gang bosses threatened to "knife the senior officers one time".

Speaking to journalists this morning at the Americans' head office in Manenberg, spokesman Dikderm Fielies said that the arrival of the Roosevelt last week had excited the gang, until they discovered that the crew were claiming to be Americans.
"Apart from being gross infringement of established gang copyright, it's just rude," said Fielies.

He said that gang bosses had immediately ordered a drive-by shooting to assert the Americans' claim to the bay.

However, he said, the strike had not been as effective as they had hoped, as Loverboy February's speedboat had been confiscated by Cape Nature Conservation a month ago and the assault team had been forced to use Uncle Salie's rowing boat.

He confirmed that the team had fired approximately 80 rounds at the "imposter Americans".

However, the sea had been very rough, he said, and 76 of the 80 rounds had gone through the bottom of the rowing boat, compelling the assault team to "effect a strategic beaching manoeuvre" which involved hanging onto driftwood until they were swept ashore at Monwabisi Beach in False Bay.

He described the shooting as a setback, but said the gang had been undaunted and had immediately summoned its "brains trust" from where it had been watching WWE Smackdown on etv in the upstairs poolroom.

"Basically they came up with two options for sinking the Roosevelt," explained Fielies.

"Pump it full of cement from Uncle Salie's wholesale building firm in Lavender Hill, or fill its hull with Late Harvest crackling and throw a Zippo down a hatch."

He said that ultimately both options had proved impracticable, and they had finally settled on a simpler, more effective plan.

"Yesterday morning Operation Roosevelt se Ma se P**s was launched," he said.

"Having borrowed another rowing boat from Jollyboy Adams, the assault team approached the Roosevelt under cover of cigarette smoke, and scratched 'Roosevelt se ma se p**s' just above its waterline.

"At the same time our operations centre on Uncle Salie's couch sent the captain of the ship a message via MXit threatening him and his crew with immediate knifing, one time."

He said the operation had been a "resounding success" as nine hours later the ship had weighed anchor and left the bay.

Meanwhile the Roosevelt's commanding officer, Captain Buck Turgidson, said he was not aware of any threats.

However, he confirmed that the dorsal gun batteries had informed him that a rowing boat full of "rustic-looking fellows had pulled up alongside yelling what sounded like 'Yo mamma's Porsche'".

"I assumed they were gentle fisher-folk enjoying some local humour," said Turgidson. "Otherwise we probably would have machine-gunned the boat, and then machine-gunned any survivors in the water."

HOROSCOPE

Aquarius Jan 20 - Feb 18

Your doctor has never seen one that big, but don't panic. There's no reason to let it change your daily routine. Except you might want to put a paper bag over it, just so passing women and children stop screaming.

www.hayibo.com

MOTLANTHE CHOSEN FOR ABILITY TO STROKE BEARD JUST LIKE MBEKI

PRETORIA. ANC members and opposition parties have welcomed the appointment of Kgalema Motlanthe as interim President, saying that his little white beard will help ease the transition between Thabo Mbeki and Jacob Zuma. Meanwhile Zuma has confirmed that it was Motlanthe's beard, and his ability to stroke it in a reassuring manner, that won him the coveted position.

The appointment of Motlanthe has calmed many South Africans who were in shock after the weekend's dramatic resignation by Mbeki, a move many analysts believe was triggered by persistent allegations that Mbeki's white beard was starting to look threadbare.

Mbeki's beard first came to prominence during negotiations with the Nationalist regime in Dakar in 1987, when then State President PW Botha was so impressed by its fine texture and resolute springiness that he tried to grow one himself.

The attempt was unsuccessful, and Botha reportedly tried to hide the failure by shaving off the lush moustache of his Minister of Foreign Affairs, Pik Botha, and gluing it onto his own chin as a beard substitute.

Mbeki's beard was once again in the headlines in 1992 when it was widely credited with ending the threat of a right-wing insurgency against democratic elections. In a meeting with AWB leader Eugene Terre'blanche, Mbeki's beard impressed with its distinguished streaks of grey, while Terre'blanche's beard was widely condemned for looking like a pubic wig stapled to his jowls.

Speaking to the media in Pretoria this morning, ANC spokesman Handpuppet Mxenge denied that there was bad blood between Mbeki and Zuma.

"Just because Comrade Mbeki has a slightly moth-eaten beard and Comrade Zuma has a sexy hot-chocolate dome and the skin of a man half his age doesn't mean that they are not both committed to the revolution," said Mxenge.

He said that Mbeki remained a valued member of the ANC, whose talents as an academic and intellectual would be invaluable when the time came "to tutor our next Youth League President in his quest to pass Grade 9 on the second try".

Meanwhile Zuma has deflected questions about his own clean-shaven appearance, saying that he did not want to detract from Motlanthe's beard.

"Every single cadre in the ANC is capable of growing a beard," he said.

Asked if this applied to women cadres as well, he said that he refused to discriminate.

However, he said he would be "very surprised if they couldn't" and urged Speaker Baleka Mbete to grow a "real old-school Moses tash just to prove the racists wrong".

search results related to: kgalema goatee

OTHER BREAKING NEWS

★ **Obama crushes children's dreams of being first black president**

★ **SA President apologizes for shoddy quality of Dalai Lama lies**

www.hayibo.com

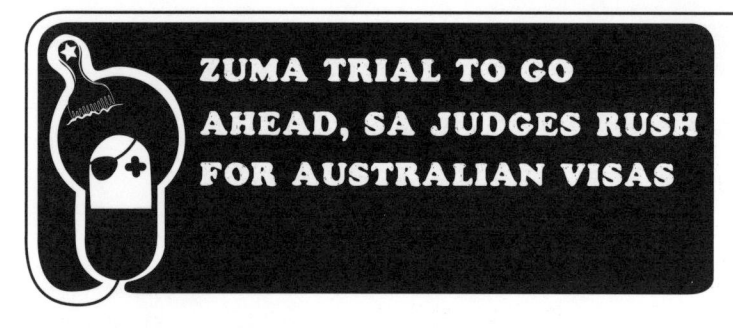

ZUMA TRIAL TO GO AHEAD, SA JUDGES RUSH FOR AUSTRALIAN VISAS

PRETORIA. The Australian Consulate in Pretoria has confirmed that it has been "overrun" by South African judges applying for citizenship after yesterday's ruling by the Supreme Court of Appeal which found that Jacob Zuma can be tried for corruption. According to Australian officials, the "poor little bastards looked absolutely terrified of getting the big gig".

"We got the first call about ninety seconds after the judgement," said Consulate official Butch Codpiece.

"He was trying to play it cool, the poor little bugger. Asking things like, 'Hypothetically, if a person were interested in moving to Australia today, without any luggage, and possibly without his family or any money, depending on how long his wife took at the ATM, but that person was a judge with twenty years at the bench, how would one go about getting the necessary forms?'"

He said that a stream of calls had quickly turned to a deluge, and that judges had started arriving at the Consulate in person, many with their possessions in bundles on their heads.

"It was pretty chaotic, just cooking stoves and goats and legal books all over our lobby," said Codpiece. "Quite a few were just sitting quietly and having a little cry, blowing their noses into their wigs."

He said that some of the judges seemed "particularly highly strung".

"One of them asked me what would happen if his application for citizenship was denied. I told him what my Mum told me in my fourth year of Grade 9: 'If at first you don't succeed, try, try again.'

"The poor bastard just started shaking and gibbering, snot flying everywhere, and then he threw up on my shoes.

"When we'd cleaned me off and hosed him down in the dipping pens out back he apologized and said he couldn't take the idea of trying Mr Zuma over and over again."

Codpiece said that while he understood the pressure the judges were under, and didn't envy them having to retry Mr Zuma in an election year, it was unlikely that any of their applications would be successful.

However, he said the etiquette of international diplomacy remained in place and that he had given all the judges a standard official Australian diplomatic response.

"I told them that the Australian people would be buggered dead and left to rot in a swamp if it would allow a bunch of girlyboys in dresses and white wigs to set foot on God's own red dust just because they're too queer to man up and send that black chappie to jail, you know, that one with the wide-apart eyes, Jacob Whatsisname."

ANC DEFENDS DISBANDING SCORPIONS TO EASE SAPS CASELOAD

PRETORIA. The ANC says the disbanding of the Scorpions will help prop up a police force buckling under a spiralling caseload. According to the Ministry of Safety and Security there are 138,000 police officers in the country, of whom 137,000 are dedicated to clearing roads and pavements ahead of ANC motorcades, leaving only 1,000 offers to fight crime.

Speaking at a ministerial lekgotla called 'Criminals: Are They Really All Bad or Are They Just Potential ANC Youth League Cadres?', Deputy Minister of Safety and Security Harpic Ntsebeza said it was no longer viable to give a unit like the Scorpions special treatment.

"It is completely unacceptable that these alleged crime-fighters sit in offices in comfy chairs, reading evidence and interviewing suspects, while the brave men and pretty girls of the SA Police Service face the dangers of limousine escort patrols," said Ntsebeza.

He explained that these dangers included "getting out of breath, tripping over an orange safety cone and being crushed under the weight of a colleague, and being looked at in a hostile manner by members of the public who don't understand what a privilege it is to be stopped for ten minutes at a traffic intersection to allow a Party limousine to come through".

www.hayibo.com

He added that the remaining 1,000 officers not currently on limousine duty were "not making immediate inroads into the criminal element", but commended them for their dedication.

"The surviving officers, and those not actively hijacking cars or blowing up ATMs, are doing fantastic work for their communities."

Earlier this year ANC secretary-general Gwede Mantashe was widely quoted in the media as saying it was "ridiculous" that the Scorpions had 600 investigators to follow up 325 cases per year.

However, he and other ANC officials have refused to comment on the Scorpions' conviction rate, which is approximately 8,000 percent higher than Police success rates.

But Ntsebeza broached the issue at the briefing.

"The public needs to understand something. Good policing is not about convictions. It's about dockets. Visible dockets.

"The more dockets there are, stacked in piles around police stations and spilling out filing cabinets and onto the floor, the safer the public feels." ✪

search results related to: saps

SA MURDERERS RECOGNIZE "DECENT EFFORT" BY ISRAELI ARMY IN GAZA

JOHANNESBURG. South Africa's cohort of murderers has sent the Israeli military a telegram of congratulation for managing to kill 1,000 people in twenty days, the same rate at which murders occur in South Africa. In the telegram the murderers hailed a "really decent effort" but warned Israel that if it wanted to compete it would need to sustain the killing all year.

Israel has been killing people at a rate of 50 per day in Gaza since its incursion began three weeks ago, and this morning South Africa's murderers said that the Israelis had done "very well" to edge ahead of South Africa's official murder rate of 49.3 people per day.

However, they agreed that beginner's luck was a factor.

"Yes, they've got that extra 0.7 on us at the moment," said murderer spokesman Slang Booi. "But let's see if they can sustain it for the rest of the year."

He said they had sent the telegram of congratulation "because everybody is always breaking down the self-esteem of murderers, and we need to stick together".

But he warned that Israel was making basic errors.

"The whole point of murdering, apart from killing people, is to stay out of the spotlight so you can keep on murdering," he said, adding that Israel was showing "considerable naivety" by using air strikes and artillery in Gaza.

"That just riles people up," said Booi, adding that if South Africa's murderers had also been using helicopter gunships the country "probably wouldn't have got the 2010 Soccer World Cup".

"I mean, you wouldn't hold the World Cup in Gaza right now, would you? And yet we've got the same body count as them. But the big difference is we use axes and rusty 9-mils. They use white phosphorus."

He said that the other major mistake Israel was making was that it had killed men.

"That's a no-no. If you really want to stay under the radar like us, you've got to kill women.

"Wives, girlfriends, sisters, sisters' daughters. Politicians have shown they don't really care if women get killed.

"So from our side, from one 50-a-day bro to another, we would urge them to dig deep, give 110 percent, lay off the men, and learn how to swing an axe." ✪

MISS WORLD TO INCLUDE COOKING, CLEANING, 'CARNAL NASTINESS'

JOHANNESBURG. The organizers of the Miss World pageant say it is time to be more honest about the agendas behind the extravaganza, and have announced that this year's winner will be the anorexic heterosexual girl in high heels who is best able to clean a home, have her husband's dinner ready on time, and perform 'carnal nastiness' on him while he reads a magazine.

Founder and patron of the pageant, former plastic surgeon turned tanningbed mogul Ramon 'The Orgasm' Velasquez, said he was delighted that the event was taking place in Johannesburg this year.

"We didn't want to go to Mexico City or Ulan Bator anyway," he said. "Africa was right up there on our list, and boy are we glad that the top seven all turned us away!"

He said that all the girls were delighted with their stables, and that each had received fresh straw and a sugar cube on arrival.

"Obviously we had to confiscate the sugar cubes," he said. "We want our public to see beautiful women, not bloated heifers. But the straw was a lovely touch."

He said that this year's pageant was themed around Transparency.

"This means two things. One, we want to be honest and open about why we stage beauty pageants, and their role in the modern, post-feminist world.

"And two, they're going to wear transparent swimsuits. It's awesome. You can see nipples and everything."

He said that it was time to "stop beating around the bush" about the sexual agendas and power dynamics behind the show.

"Women are confused about their roles in a modern globalised world," he said. "Our job as pageant wranglers is to reassure them that they are still as prized as ever: as homemakers, as cooks, as cleaners, and most importantly as willing performers of carnal nastiness on their husband when he comes home after a long tiring day at the golf course."

However, he categorically denied that the changes were in any way an admission that beauty pageants were about objectifying women.

"These are strong women who reflect their strength through their hair, fingernails, and how far they can tilt their heads over onto one shoulder while listening to the judges' questions.

"In fact we think of the pageant as a symbol of their liberation. We're celebrating women's freedom. They're free to pursue any job they want, whether that is a secretary, the curator of a gallery bought for them by their husbands, or housewives, because we all know that's the hardest job in the world."

Asked why the pageant and others like it did not feature openly gay women, Velasquez said that gay people were "sexually rapacious and loose and would hit on anything with a pulse", which might disturb "less perverted contestants".

He added that fat women were also excluded because while they were beautiful on the inside, "beauty pageants are about what's spray-painted and glued to the outside".

search results related to: miss world cooking

SOARING FOOD PRICES HURT WORLD'S POOR, REALLY HURT WORLD'S FAT

ATLANTA. As food prices continue to climb, the world's fat have called upon governments to address the crisis before they have to resort to eating household pets, homeless people, or, in extreme cases, vegetables. According to a spokesman, the fat are "tired, stressed, and want a cookie, now." Latest figures suggest that this would require 1.3 billion cookies.

Recent surges in the price of staple foodstuffs such as rice and wheat have crippled the world's poor, but the world's fat say they too are victims of rampant global food inflation.

"We eat rice too," said spokesman for the fat, Marty Erickson, of Atlanta, Georgia. "And wheat. We eat everything.

"I guarantee, any crappy scrawny little grain a poor person eats, we've eaten it first. The poor do not have a monopoly on hunger."

Erickson said that it was time for world leaders to take "drastic, pragmatic, and trans-fat-enriched action" to prevent a wave of "binge violence" by the planet's 1.3 billion overweight inhabitants.

He said that the world's fat condemned reports of fat people hunting in packs, killing and eating overweight homeless people or particularly plump household pets.

However, he said, "desperate times call for desperate measuring cups".

"We would never condone the senseless slaying and spit-roasting of a homeless person, even if that homeless person had been well basted, and had somehow contrived to die with an apple in their mouth.

"Likewise, if I were to stumble across my neighbour's miniature potbelly pig, say late at night, in my driveway, and I accidentally flipped the pig onto my barbecue, which I had absentmindedly lit a little earlier; and if I were to fall face down onto the pig, over and over again, until I had unwittingly ingested all of it, I would feel just terrible.

"But that's what we do. We eat, and we feel terrible, so I guess I'd get over it."

He also called on the governments of the United States and the European Union to halt the planting of wheat for use in artificial fuels, one of the prime drivers of recent food inflation.

"No carbs for oil! No carbs for oil!" he shouted, before being hospitalized for an irregular heartbeat. ✪

PIGGY-BANK BLASTS INCREASE AS ATM BOMBERS SETTLE DOWN, START FAMILIES

PRETORIA. Police say they have seen a dramatic increase in the number of piggy-banks blown up, with upward of 20 heists a week reported in day-care centres in Gauteng. "A lot of ATM bombers are settling down and starting families," said a spokesman. "Armed robbery is a growth industry in this country, so it's natural they're encouraging their kids to learn the trade."

ATM bombings have dominated headlines in recent weeks, with 270 blown up by criminals and 183 blown up by irate bank customers after having their debit cards swallowed.

However, police say the spate of piggy-bank blasts is a new phenomenon that reflects the newfound financial security of South African criminals.

"More and more former ATM bombers are investing their earnings in quiet, middle-class lifestyles," said police spokesman Capt. Buksie Grensvegter.

"They're settling down, buying a home in the suburbs, having kids, and obviously passing on their skills to the next generation."

Estate agent Debbi Remora confirmed the trend, saying that she had seen a spike in the number of clients "with a Grade 6 education, some training in either the South African or Zimbabwean military, and a suitcase full of slightly singed banknotes", looking for "somewhere leafy near a good daycare centre".

Meanwhile the police are urging day-mothers and kindergarten teachers to be on the lookout for toddlers acting suspiciously.

"That means kiddies who are moody, or are playing apart from the group, or are bringing plastic explosive to show-and-tell in their lunchboxes," said Grensvegter.

"Also, we are appealing to adult caregivers not to provoke these children by exposing them to cash or jewellery, piggy-banks, collections tins, and so on."

He said people needed to understand that the children of ATM bombers had "special needs".

"When you combine a child's natural curiosity with a general sense of entitlement and the ability to use complex detonators, you have a potentially upsetting situation," said Grensvegter.

Asked what the police were doing in the interim to curb ATM bombings, he said, "Ag, you know, the normal.

"Park under bridges, eat pepper-steak pies, pull over white female undergraduates and fine them for having too little tread on their tyres. You know. Policing." ✪

www.hayibo.com

MBOWENI OPEN TO THIRD TERM AFTER 28 PERCENT PAY RISE

PRETORIA. Reserve Bank Governor Tito Mboweni has confirmed that he is open to serving a third term after he received a 28 percent pay rise this year. Mboweni's salary is now reportedly R3.8 million a year, or roughly equivalent to what a teacher earns in 27 years and a police constable in 40. "It's a dirty job," he said, "but someone's got to step up and take one for the team."

"Or take 3.8 million ones for the team, as the case may be."

Speaking to journalists this morning in Pretoria, Mboweni said that he had not yet made a final decision over his future but would make an announcement once he had carefully considered his options.

It is believed most of his options are stock options in BEE companies with government contracts to build, demolish and rebuild public toilets in the Karoo.

Mboweni conceded that he had sometimes got tired of earning his previous salary, which was R2.9 million a year, and had at times yearned to "just be an ordinary Member of Parliament, spending weekends throwing empty whisky bottles over the wall, shredding wire-tap transcripts and doing donuts in my Beemer".

However, he said that he had stayed on in the job out of a sense of duty, and because nobody else in the country, or indeed the world, could do what he did.

"Being Governor of the Reserve Bank is incredibly complicated," he said. "But fortunately I am almost supernaturally clever.

"Anyone other than myself who tried to do this would die instantaneously.

"They would whimper and then their heads would explode."

Asked why inflation was running at 12 percent while he was being paid R3.8 million a year to keep it between 3 and 6 percent, he explained that "numerous forces were at work".

He named these as "the Americans – both the superpower and the Cape Flats gang – oil, wheat, Helen Zille, the big machine they're building under Alaska that can control the weather, Helen Zille, malaria, space chimps, and obviously Helen Zille".

He also used the opportunity to announce that he would no longer be referring to himself as part of South African society in future statements.

"I cannot in good conscience continue to say things like 'We must all strive to tighten our belts as we face some severe economic challenges'," he said.

"I need to be honest with myself and with you, and let you know that from now on, you're on your own.

"So to recap: you need to tighten your belts, and you need to face some severe economic challenges, while I bathe in dachshund milk and have my scalp Botoxed."

The press conference ended on a sour note when one journalist asked him if he was turning into a fat cat.

A furious Mboweni denied that he was fat, insisting that he was "just big-boned" before storming out.

search results related to: fat cat

WHITE SOUTH AFRICA TORN APART BY HOFMEYR-HUISGENOOT ROW

PRETORIA. Trauma counsellors say white South Africans are being "torn apart inside" by the feud between Steve Hofmeyr and 'Huisgenoot' editor Esmaré Weideman. Hofmeyr emptied a cup of tea over Weideman's head earlier this week, causing millions of white South Africans to run to their room, lock the door, and beg Mammie and Pappie to stop fighting.

The incident, which received widespread media coverage, took place at a restaurant at the Lost Palace in Sun City during the Miss South Africa pageant. According to organizers, both Hofmeyr and Weideman had been invited as they both embodied the style, class and sophistication that Sun City and the pageant represented. Reports in the national media suggest Hofmeyr walked up to Weideman and emptied a cup of cold tea over her head.

It is not yet clear whether this was a response to a series of articles in 'Huisgenoot' about his infidelities, or whether it was a statement about the gutter press in general and photo essays about one anorexic's quest for lasting love with her childhood sweetheart after his face was reconstructed after being chewn off by a pitbull terrier on his parents' smallholding on the East Rand.

According to witnesses, the tea was cold because Hofmeyr had spent most of the morning glaring at Weideman while trying to think of something cutting to say to her.

"He wrote down about twenty options on a napkin," said Lost Palace guest Chrizelda Voorlaaier.

"At first he was going to say, 'Hello, Esmaré, you must be Joko-ing', but he probably thought it was too subtle and would go straight over the head of someone who edits 'Huisgenoot'."

According to Voorlaaier, Hofmeyr finally settled on "Nobody writes crapper articles than you and Five Roses", although it is unknown whether or not he actually said this while dribbling the cold tea over Weideman's perm.

Meanwhile the row has pulled the rug out from under white South Africans, and trauma counsellors across the country say they have been swamped with pleas from desperate whites who feel that the moral and cultural foundations of their world are crumbling.

"Steve Hofmeyr and 'Huisgenoot' are the Alpha and Omega for millions of white people in this country," said counsellor Cadenza Mbete. "In many ways they are parent figures."

She said that "Father Steve" and "Mother Huisgenoot" had taught white South Africa most of what it knew.

"He taught us that the sky is the limit as long as you leak your personal life to the media at strategic moments and do a middling Neil Diamond impression.

"And 'Huisgenoot' taught us that most of the country's problems are caused by Satanists and feminists, and that the two greatest moments in any woman's life are when she produces her first son and self-publishes her first book of inspiration poems."

She said that when these two "primal caregivers and mentors" fought, the trauma would be immense.

"It's just so sad," she said. "So incredibly sad."

search results related to: sad hofmeyr

CHARLTON HESTON DIES OF ALZHEIMER'S, NATIONAL RIFLE ASSOCIATION VINDICATED

LOS ANGELES. Hollywood legend and pro-gun lobbyist Charlton Heston died on the weekend of an Alzheimer's related illness. He was 84. A spokesman for the National Rifle Association, which Heston chaired until 2003, said he hoped that the star's death would "prove once and for all that guns don't kill people – old age kills people."

Heston, who rose to fame in the late 1950s as a square-jawed all-American leading man dealing out justice to helmeted gorillas, Pharisees and craven idols, was best known by younger generations as an outspoken defender of Americans' right to bear arms.

As chairman of the influential National Rifle Association, Heston was largely responsible for passing 1989's Self Defense Bill in Congress, which allowed hunters to carry multi-barrelled water-cooled belt-fed artillery loaded with explosive armour-piercing rounds, in case they were confronted "in a menacing way by the local fauna".

The bill was amended in 1990 when minority rights activists persuaded lawmakers to reclassify Native Americans, Russian and Japanese immigrants, Jews and nature conservationists as "local people" rather than "local fauna".

He also made headlines when he famously told an NRA convention: "You can take my rifle – when you pry it from my cold dead hands!"

According to current NRA chairman Cletus Schwartz, Heston's rifle has not yet been prised from his cold dead hands.

He said that the star's death should be the end of the debate over personal weaponry in the United States.

"We've always said that guns don't kill people. People kill people," he told reporters this morning. "But I think we also need to recognize that dementia kills people too."

He added that the NRA was certain that further research would prove that up to 87 percent of civilian casualties in Iraq were due to Alzheimer's and similar conditions.

Heston's film career spanned over forty years and included 1959's gay sex romp 'Ben-Hur', 1968's gay sex romp 'Planet of the Apes', and 1971's gay sex romp, 'The Omega Man'.

He leaves behind a wife, three children, seven grandchildren, and 57,000 rounds of full metal jacket ammunition.

search results related to: gay sex romp

MANUEL URGES SA TO SAVE A LITTLE BIT OF MINUS NOTHING

PRETORIA. Finance Minister Trevor Manuel has again urged South Africans to save. Manuel conceded that most citizens had no actual money to save, having been taxed to a point where they were eating boiled shoes, but he said that people should try to "put a little something away every month, to get into the habit, even if that something is just a dead squirrel".

The Minister's call came a day after new shock figures revealed that South Africa has a negative savings rate.

"It's quite complicated," said Manuel, "but essentially what this means is that people are saving, but they're depositing less than nothing.

"As far as we can tell, they are going to banks with small amounts of anti-matter."

Asked if this meant that South Africans were depositing tiny black holes, Manuel said he did not want to attach racist labels to complex scientific concepts.

"We prefer to call them previously disadvantaged holes," said Manuel.

www.hayibo.com

Manuel's most recent calls on South Africans to save have been met with incredulous silence by most citizens, who pay tax on the tax the government extracts from taxable savings, not including the tax paid on the tax paid on the tax levied for breathing South African air, which is considered a taxable asset by the government.

Most citizens currently earn enough to buy one second-hand Bata Toughie school shoe per month, which is generally boiled with garlic and rice and feeds a family for three weeks.

According to Manuel, this was good news for potential savers.

"If you can afford a Bata Toughie then you can definitely afford to scale down to a Chinese knock-off, like a Barta Tuffie, and use the left-over funds to save," he said.

He asked South Africans to look to biblical role models.

"Jesus was the simple son of a carpenter, with only a limited income as a motivational speaker," said Manuel.

"And yet the church tells us that He saved millions."

search results related to: trevor manuel

HOROSCOPE

Cancer - Jun 22 - Jul 22

Remember, a bird in the hand is worth two in the bush. But a bird in the hand can also make it difficult to brush your teeth or type up important documents. Weigh up your bird options carefully.

SASOL COMMITTED TO ART, JUST NOT ART FEATURING PENISES

JOHANNESBURG. Oil giant Sasol says it remains committed to supporting South African artists but has urged them to create work more in line with Sasol's ethos of complete corporate subjugation of free will. The statement follows weekend revelations that the winner of this year's Sasol New Signatures art competition had upset the company's employees by showing a glimpse of a penis.

'Familieportret No 2', a photograph by artist Richard Strydom, also featured a young woman baring one of her breasts. However Sasol spokesman Pieter-Willem Botha said that staff had had no problem with the breast. "We at Sasol accept that all art is ultimately about looking at naked women," he told the media this morning.

"There is nothing more natural than a nice big breast pinned up on a cubicle wall or in a workshop, or slipped into your desk drawer." He added that he was "obviously talking about a picture of a breast and not a real breast" as it would contravene health and safety regulations to pin a real breast to a cubicle wall.

However, he said, the penis featured in the photograph had been too much for many at Sasol's head office. "For most of our male employees the penis represents frustration, disappointment and failure," said Botha. "And for our female employees it pretty much means the same."

He said that Sasol would continue to sponsor the New Signatures competition to help identify and nurture artistic talent, but hoped that artists would enter more appropriate pieces next year.

"Obviously we're not going to dictate form and content," said Botha. "But if entrants are unsure, perhaps a useful guideline might be to aim at the sort of thing that the members of our board have in their homes."

He said these included bronze sculptures of leopards drinking at watering holes, photo-realistic paintings of lovable black urchins playing soccer, "and obviously lots of stuff by the doyen of bespoke domestic art, Carrol Boyes".

"In fact we are hoping that Carrol enters Sasol New Signatures next year," he added. "Maybe with a big set of salad spoons that can represent the past and the future of South Africa, coming together to load the lettuce of harmony and the feta cheese of forgiveness onto the Boardmans crockery of democracy.

"Or something lekker arty like that."

THE DEVIL MADE ME DO IT, SAYS LONE VIEWER OF HANSIE MOVIE

BLOEMFONTEIN. The only person known to have paid money to see Hansie: The Movie says he was tricked by Satan. Hempies Smit, 28, of Brakpan, says he had no intention of seeing the film about former cricket captain Hansie Cronje, but was overcome by demonic forces at the box office. Smit is believed to have seen the entire film and is currently in a critical but stable condition.

Speaking to journalists from his bed at the Gé Korsten Memorial Hospital in Bloemfontein where he is being treated for severe nausea and diarrhoea brought on by prolonged exposure to the film, Smit said that he had gone to the cinema intending to watch something else, but that "dark forces" had made him buy a ticket to 'Hansie'.

"The lady behind the counter went a bit pale, which was hectic because she was Sesotho, and she asked me if I was sure because nobody else in the country has paid their own money to see it," recalled Smit.

Describing the film as "diabolical", he confirmed that its tagline – "How do you start over once you've betrayed a nation's trust?" – was in fact a reference to Cronje's deception and not, as widely believed, a reference to the film's scriptwriter and director.

Smit said that he was still somewhat disoriented by the experience, but remembered being simultaneously overwhelmed by "intense boredom and an urgent need to run away". However, he said, he had remained in his seat "because by that stage Beelzebub was calling the shots".

However, Smit said he was trying to remain positive about the ordeal. "Look, it's a solid film, for a movie made to exonerate a deceased icon by his brother targeting a straight-to-DVD market in rural South Africa," said Smit. "To be fair there were only a handful of weak aspects."

He said that these had included the script, the directing, the camera work, the acting, and lighting and the editing. "But for the rest it was fine," he said.

He had special praise for Sarah Thompson, the American actress who plays Cronje's Afrikaans wife Bertha, saying that Thompson had brought "genuine nuance to the role with her American German Cockney impression of Keira Knightley sitting on a carrot".

He said the film's other actresses had not had a chance to shine as their roles were limited to walking into the kitchen to prepare food for the men, or walking out of the kitchen having prepared food for the men.

Meanwhile the film's distributors have confirmed that Grey College in Bloemfontein has bought a print and will be showing it non-stop to its pupils for the next 300 years to remind them that nothing is wrong as long as you're forgiven by adolescent boys at your old high school.

search results related to: hansie lying

CONFUSED SOUTH AFRICANS ASK COPE WHERE E CAME FROM

JOHANNESBURG. As the breakaway Congress of the People, or COPE, celebrates its official launch, confused and frightened South Africans are asking party leadership to explain where the 'e' comes from in its acronym and wondering whether a party that can't identify which letters appear in its name can be trusted to run an entire country.

The newly formed Congress of the People named itself after the so-called Congress of the People in 1955, a Congress where People Congressed with other People.

However, the acronym of the party's name as represented in its official logo is not COP but COPE.

This morning constitutional expert Abacus Nyamende explained that there were three possible reasons for the inclusion of the 'e' at the end of the acronym.

"Either they don't understand what an acronym is, or they are keeping an extra word starting with 'e' secret from the electorate, or they are severely mentally handicapped," he said.

"Given that they are all ANC members trying to convince the electorate that they are offering a completely new party with original policies, we might be looking at severe mental defects here.

"However, one also can't rule out that because they are essentially ANC politicians, it might also be possible that they are extremely intelligent and sophisticated while believing that the electorate is severely mentally handicapped."

He said it was also unlikely that COPE's leadership didn't know what an acronym was, as the entire liberation struggle had been based on a series of acronyms.

"You can't come out of a culture that gave us SASCO, COSATU, the UDF, SASQUATCH, POEPHOL, PUSTULE and all the other great movements, and not know how to construct an acronym."

He said the likeliest scenario was that the party's name included a word beginning with 'e' that would only be revealed after the election so as not to scare off potential voters.

"You might find they're actually called 'Congress of the People's Enema' or something like that," said Nyamende.

He said it was nothing to be worried about, as the ANC had been giving the country an enema for over a decade and that "a change of personnel around the hose" might be what the country needed.

search results related to: enema

OUSTED MUGABE LIKELY TO BE TRIED FOR "HORRIFIC" DRESS SENSE

HARARE. The International Criminal Court in The Hague has confirmed that if Robert Mugabe is ousted from power in Zimbabwe, it will seek to try him for "sustained and brutal" crimes against fashion. According to an ICC spokesman, it was time that Mr Mugabe "faced the music for conducting a brutal thirty-year campaign of sartorial terrorism."

With many votes still to be counted – and even more yet to be burned by the Zimbabwean Defence Force's Democracy Squad – it was unclear this morning whether or not Mugabe's stranglehold on the country was loosening.

However, what has emerged is a clear intent by international lawmakers to bring Mugabe to justice for what they call crimes against fashion.

"Mugabe's excesses need no introduction," said chief prosecutor Jean Valjean. "We are all familiar with the shocking images over the years.

"The long-sleeved nylon shirts bearing a pixellated photograph of the dictator's own face. The trousers always a fraction too short, revealing just a flash of Shoprite-bought nylon socks. And of course then there are the spectacles."

Senior prosecutor Gysbert Gouda agreed that Mugabe's heavy-rimmed spectacles were "possibly the most disturbing accessory to a fashion crime" the court had ever witnessed.

"No doubt the accused will claim that he did not know how offensive his glasses were," said Gouda. "But ignorance of the laws of accessorizing is no excuse.

"Surely, as he flicked a tsetse fly off his electric green baseball cap and buttoned his double-breasted blazer he stopped to consider that the only people who wear this sort of spectacles are the kind who loiter in late-night adult video viewingbooths?"

Meanwhile a defiant Mugabe has rejected calls that he hand himself over to the ICC.

"I am what I am," he told reporters outside his compound. "I don't want praise, I don't want pity. I bang my own drum. Some think it's noise, I think it's pretty.

"And so what if I love each sparkle and each bangle? Why not see things from a different angle? Your life is a sham 'til you can shout out, 'I am what I am!'"

www.hayibo.com

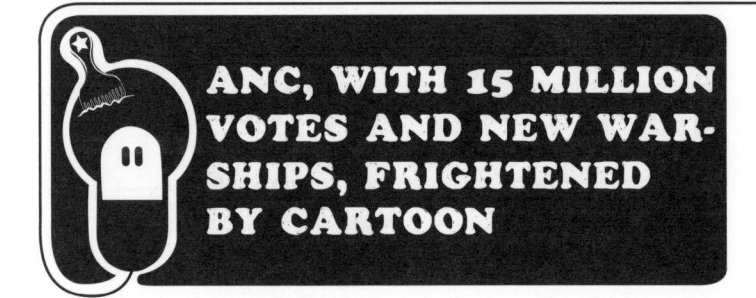

ANC, WITH 15 MILLION VOTES AND NEW WARSHIPS, FRIGHTENED BY CARTOON

PRETORIA. Party insiders have confirmed that despite having a guaranteed two-thirds majority in the next election, the entire GDP at its disposal, R30-billion worth of high-tech weaponry, and complete control of the national broadcaster, the ANC has been "badly frightened" by a controversial cartoon by Jonathan Shapiro depicting the rape of South Africa's justice system by Jacob Zuma.

The cartoon appeared over the weekend in the 'Sunday Times' and immediately unleashed a storm of activity at the ANC's headquarters in Luthuli House, where an alert level of 'Mshini Wami 4' was declared.

It was the first time Luthuli House has gone to 'Mshini Wami 4', the previous highest being 'Mshini Wami 2', declared in 2006 after Zuma had his account with Amazon.com suspended over late payment for a consignment of books which included the collected works of Freud and an illustrated beginner's guide to the work of Germaine Greer.

Addressing the Luthuli House press corps this morning, party spokesman Doughnut Phiri said that Shapiro needed to be "eliminated, destroyed or killed, both literally and/or metaphorically and/or metaphysically, or whichever one we are allowed to do by the Human Rights Commission".

Asked why the ANC and its allies had chosen to present an outraged united front against a solitary cartoonist rather than against Aids, crime, or the abuse of women, Phiri said that Shapiro was "more dangerous than Aids, criminals and women combined".

He declined to explain how this was the case, but said it was "logical to everyone but racists and counterrevolutionaries".

He added that the state could still decide to pursue Shapiro "with everything at its disposal"

This included four corvettes, one manned submarine and two unmanned submarines on bricks, six Swedish fighter jets flown by pilots leased from the Botswana Air Force, an oral poet named SlamSista Mzanzi, 15 million loyal voters, and a slightly soiled copy of the Constitution.

Shapiro could not be reached for comment this morning as he is currently in New York attending a United Nations-sponsored conference called 'South African Leadership: An Oxymoron for Our Times.'

search results related to: mshini wami

2010 WORLD CUP MASCOT IS NOT ROTTING STD-RAVAGED LION

DURBAN. The local organizing committee of the 2010 World Cup has defended the tournament's new mascot, saying that it is not a moth-eaten and gangrenous lion covered in lesions caused by a sexually transmitted disease, but rather a leopard with green hair. However, it conceded that the mascot had been found in the props cupboard at the SABC, and dated from 1984.

Speaking to the media this morning from the newly renamed Comrade Jacob Zuma Long May He Shower Us with Blessings Conference Centre in Durban, LOC spokesman Laduma Vilakazi said that South Africans would learn to love the mascot, Zakumi.

"Or at least not hate it," he added, saying that South Africans had shown that "they will eventually get used to anything".

He said that Zakumi had tested well on young audiences when he first appeared on national television, in a walk-on role in 'Pumpkin Patch' in 1985 when he tried to have sex with Woofles in an episode entitled 'Woofles's Body Is Nobody's Body but Woofles's'.

He said criticism that Zakumi looked embarrassingly out of date were "unfair and hurtful to many people, especially the designer and the designer's mother."

www.hayibo.com

"We know that Zakumi isn't exactly a cutting-edge mascot," said Vilakazi.

"We know that modern mascots are stylized, full of moulded features and articulated limbs, and not just someone zipped up inside a big nylon animal with a bobble-head."

But, he said, the LOC had felt it was important to have a mascot from the mid-1980s to "remind everyone that Africa is twenty years behind the rest of the world, and that they owe us big-time".

"Obviously we want fans to enjoy the football, but we also want them to understand that their political and economic system raped our continent," he said.

"We want them to have fun in South Africa while still feeling overwhelming shame for their role in funding Apartheid."

He said that Zakumi was therefore "all about guilt, shame and self-loathing, but in a very forward-thinking and optimistic way".

He also confirmed that the mascot's name had had to be changed after an "unpleasant scene that required an exorcist to intervene".

"As we explained to the media at the launch, the 'ZA' in Zakumi represents ZA or South Africa, and the 'kumi' means 'ten' in many African languages.

"Originally we were just going to go for 'SA' and 'Ten', or Saten, but it didn't work out."

He said a test run at a Catholic primary school in Durban had "ended badly" after 500 children began chanting, "I love Saten! I love Saten!"

Meanwhile football pundits have welcomed the mascot, saying it perfectly represents the national team since leopards spend most of their time having their trophies stolen by stronger predators or sleeping in trees.

search results related to: 2010 mascot

NON-DISABLED NON-ATHLETES DEMAND OWN OLYMPICS

BEIJING. As the Paralympic Games continue in Beijing, uncoordinated and unmotivated people are demanding their own Olympics. "If you're giving Olympic medals to physically disabled people, you have to give them to people who are depressed, comatose, or simply not very athletic," said a lobbyist, adding that it was time to stop discriminating against the non-disabled.

Human rights lawyers agree. According to advocate Izzy Cheesecake of 'Off the Couch and Onto the Podium', an action group championing the cause of sedentary Olympic hopefuls, the Paralympics are deeply discriminatory against non-disabled non-athletes.

"There are thousands of reasons why people can't be awarded a gold medal in the 100-metre sprint at the Olympic Games," he told journalists this morning.

"You might be an amputee, or have cerebral palsy. But you also might be too slow, or too fat, or you might have to work late that evening. You might have an upset stomach. Or you promised the kids you'd go to their school play.

"Disabilities are just a tiny fraction of all the reasons most people aren't Olympic champions."

He said that when one examined the event in this way, the decision to give disabled people an Olympics of their own, and to exclude all other possible categories of non-athletic also-rans, seemed to be "a terribly cruel and arbitrary decision".

Meanwhile lobbyists for the proposed Average Olympics say they have had overwhelming interest in various events, with the marathon sleep and the 10-metre stroll for people who just can't be arsed, proving the most popular.

"People who just can't be arsed are as deserving of a gold medal as Usain Bolt," said organiser Gladys Craw. "What this upsurge in enthusiasm shows is that people who can't be arsed are getting up and doing it for themselves."

However, she said that some events were still being debated, adding that pistol-shooting for the clinically depressed would have to be closely monitored to prevent "unpleasant scenes of self-extermination that might sour the mood of Olympic exuberance."

www.hayibo.com

ANC YOUTH LEAGUE TO DEVELOP OWN BIG BANG PARTICLE COLLIDER

PRETORIA. Inspired by the historic firing of the Large Hadron Collider in Switzerland, the ANC Youth League says it intends building a similar device to explore, at a subatomic level, the bias of the media and the judiciary against Jacob Zuma. According to a spokesman, this would be done by colliding newspaper editors and judges at close to the speed of light "to see what happens".

The ambitious project was announced this morning by ANCYL science and technology spokesman Einstein Shabangu, who is currently completing a correspondence course in wheel-alignment at the Tony Yengeni Technical University of the North West.

According to Shabangu, the proposed collider would work according to the same principles as the Large Hadron Collider in Europe, which accelerates particles to close to the speed of light in a vast underground tunnel.

"The science is beautifully simple," he said.

"We take two counterrevolutionary particles such as a racist judge and a megalomaniac newspaper editor, we strap them to gurneys, and then accelerate the gurneys to around 600 kilometres per hour, which is close to the speed of light."

He said a "vast array of scientific instruments, mostly Dictaphones and camera-phones", would monitor the particles for any useful information, such as screamed confessions of racism or evidence of witchcraft.

According to Shabangu a large number of factors would determine when the climactic collision needed to take place, including the number of spectators, the bias or racism of the particles being collided, and the quality of the free finger-snacks being served in the VIP lounge next door.

However, he said, the signal would come directly from Luthuli House.

"We imagine something dignified and stately, like Comrade Zuma dropping a silk handkerchief or slowly turning his thumbs down."

He denied that the collider would become a white elephant once all the country's judges and editors had been hosed off the walls of the machine.

"Science is a never-ending struggle," he said. "If we finish with counterrevolutionary particles we might start a new experiment, perhaps with dissident particles within the party, or ethnic particles.

"That's the wonderful thing about physics.

"It's just like the socialist revolution. It goes on forever, with an unlimited budget, and you never have to justify whether you're making any progress or not."

search results related to: gurney collider

OTHER BREAKING NEWS

★ **Gavin Hood fans demand Tsotsi-Game sequel**

★ **Manto denies new cabinet post is as bartender-chef**

www.hayibo.com

TERRIFIED SOUTH AFRICANS BEG NOT TO BE SHOWN BOK COACH SEX TAPE

CAPE TOWN. South Africans have begged the media not to show them the alleged sex tape featuring Springbok rugby coach Peter de Villiers, and human rights groups fear that millions of citizens could be "deeply scarred" by seeing footage of "a stocky middle-aged man with a handlebar moustache putting the moves on a woman in the back seat of her station-wagon".

De Villiers has fiercely denied the existence of the alleged tape, and says that the allegations are part of an ongoing campaign by racist elements in South African rugby to remove him from the coaching position.

This morning representatives of a broad range of human rights watch groups agreed that De Villiers's suspicions could not be discounted, but begged racist plotters to be more considerate towards their fellow South Africans.

"If this is a plot by white right-wingers to get rid of De Villiers, it's the lowest they've sunk," said human rights lawyer Delilah Samson.

"Lacing people's clothes with poison is one thing, but subjecting innocent law-abiding citizens to horrific, nauseating and deeply disturbing erotica is beyond the pale."

Psychologist Gaylord Steinway-Upright agreed, begging the media not to show the tape if it turns out to be real.

"South Africans are simply not equipped psychologically and emotionally to see Mr De Villiers in the nude," he said.

"Ryk Neethling, yes. Minki van der Westhuizen, yes. Those are racist plots we can deal with. But not this."

However, the regional director of Oxfam's 'Keep It in Your Pants' pilot project, Chatterley Tswete, said that she would welcome a televised glimpse of the tape as it might "go a very long way towards convincing our young people to wait before having sex, perhaps until they are 60 or 70, or as long as it takes to erase the horrific images from their minds".

A spokesman for the South African Rugby Union said that it would release a statement shortly, but was still being sidetracked by a "minor disturbance" at its head office.

"One of the board members threw an orange at another one while they were exercising on the tyre-swings this morning," said the spokesman.

"He retaliated by biting the one who had thrown the orange, and then the whole Saru executive became extremely agitated."

He said that after "some shrieking and throwing of fruit across the executive enclosure", security had arrived and been forced to dart most of the board.

However, he assured the public that the delay was temporary and that a statement would be issued as soon as the board had "slept it off".

search results related to: handlebar

OTHER BREAKING NEWS

★ ANC Youth League in turmoil over Malema Mercedes

★ Holy ANC confirms Helen Zille is the Antichrist

★ Peter Marais vows loyalty to Cope until he gets better offer

www.hayibo.com

DEMOCRATIC ALLIANCE SAYS LEADERSHIP IS AFRICAN-AMERICAN BLACK

CAPE TOWN. The Democratic Alliance says it is determined to shake off its image as a mainly white party, and has decided to adopt a colour grading system pioneered by African Americans that allows incredibly fair-skinned people to call themselves black.

According to the new system, the entire leadership of the opposition party is now black, with Joe Seremane reclassified as ultrablack.

Speaking to journalists at the party's winter compound next to the Meadowridge Park-n-Shop this morning, spokesman Niles Lebensraum admitted that the overwhelming whiteness of the DA's leadership had been "something of a handicap" in recent elections.

He said that research by DA strategists Doris Jenkins, 86, and Gladys van der Merwe, 83, had shown that black South Africans were still "wilfully and maliciously ignoring the potential benefits of white rule".

"We're not saying that those 342 years of white rule were all a picnic," said Lebensraum.

"But for God's sake, they've had 14 whole years of black rule – how much more do they want?"

However, he said, thanks to the African American system of racial classification, the black-white divide was now a thing of the past.

"African American icons like Colin Powell and Tyra Banks have shown us that you can have fair skin and still be a strong black person," said Lebensraum.

He said that the party's leadership was "thrilled" with the new classification, and confirmed that "ultrablack" Joe Seremane had spent the day walking up to colleagues, giving them high fives, and introducing himself as "megabad ultrablack supaphly life-taker and heartbreaker Hot Chocolate Joe".

He added that Helen Zille had asked Seremane to stop as it was upsetting some of the more fragile white workers in the office.

According to Lebensraum, the reclassification was an historic moment for the party, as its previous efforts at becoming more black had ended badly.

He said that Tony Leon had once spent an entire summer on a LiLo on Hartbeespoort Dam smeared with cooking oil in order to gain more credibility as a black African, but had returned to Parliament only to be mistaken for Patricia de Lille.

"The great thing about this new system is that you can be basically white, but also black, just like Colin Powell," said Lebensraum.

He added that "black" was a "broad church".

"Nobody is suggesting that Helen Zille is gunmetal-blue like some of these Congolese chappies that wash our Volvos next door at the Park-n-Shop," he said.

"Because she's not. She's more sort of honey-and-cream-ish, a lot like Tyra Banks. They have a very similar look."

He urged people to remember that "even Madiba is more yellowish than black", adding that most of the DA's leadership had thought he was Chinese after he was released.

search results related to: african american black

BOESAK TO REVIVE UDF, LEG-WARMERS, SHOULDER PADS

CAPE TOWN. Allan Boesak says his plans to launch a United Democratic Front-style party also include appropriate 1980s accessories that match the ideology and aesthetic of the movement. Speaking to journalists this morning, Boesak said that the new party would stand for non-racial democracy, human rights, leg-warmers, shoulderpads and high-top sneakers.

Boesak rose to prominence in the 1980s for his leadership in the UDF and for his exceptional break-dancing and beat-boxing skills, and by 1987 he was reviled by the apartheid security apparatus for being able to mobilize popular support in the townships while moonwalking in stone-washed jeans past police barricades.

However, the cleric fell from grace in 1999 when he was convicted of fraud, having sold a Paula Abdul mix tape to his congregation by persuading them it was Janet Jackson with a cold.

This morning Boesak said it was time to forget the past, except for the 1980s which had been radical, and to look forward to 2009.

"It was the great philosophers Milli and Vanilli who said, 'Those who forget the mistakes of the 1980s are destined to repeat them'," said Boesak.

"This country is crying out for a return to the values of the 1980s, when people were more open and honest, and when friends could do the Loco-Motion and buy a packet of chips for 33 cents."

He said that the founding tenet of his new party, and of the 1980s, was non-violence.

"The '80s made us understand that when you get angry or you're being persecuted, you don't fight.

"You dance.

"Alone, with some air-guitar to show your pain."

He said that the most effective angry-dancing was done in an abandoned factory, a barn, or an alley with steam coming out of manholes.

"South Africa's poor are angry. They have been ignored, and they are angry. They need jobs and food, but most of all they need abandoned factories and some barns so that they can express their anger in an aesthetically pleasing way."

He said that his party would be launching a major initiative next month to get scrunchies and leg-warmers into the townships.

"It is time for the voiceless to be heard," he said.

"Let the drum-pads of freedom beat, let the synthesizer of unity play the music of sweet democracy, all night long, all night, yeah, all night long, all night."

search results related to: boesak shoulderpads

PRETORIA'S FIDEL CASTRO STREET TO BE ONE-WAY CUL-DE-SAC

PRETORIA. The Tshwane council has confirmed that Pretorius Street in Pretoria is set to be renamed Fidel Castro Street, and will "celebrate the legacy" of Cuba's veteran leader. As such, the street will be transformed from a thriving thoroughfare into a one-way cul-de-sac whose residents will have access to excellent healthcare but won't be allowed to read newspapers.

The South African Communist Party has celebrated the decision, saying it has already reported the victory to the Kremlin.

"We called the Soviet Triumph Hotline as soon as we heard," said SACP spokesman Pogrom Pedi.

"As usual it went straight to answering machine, so we reported the heroism of our street-renaming cadres, and reminded the Comrades to give us our new orders."

He said that the message on the answering machine had been unchanged "for some time now", and that it said that Party leadership was away on clandestine anti-capitalist manoeuvres and "would return to Moscow in June 1989".

He also conceded that Moscow had not given the SACP any new orders since early 1987, when it had sent a postcard from Bali which read, "Wish you were here, weather great, just keep on, you know, being angry about the exploitation of the etc etc".

He said that the creation of Fidel Castro Street would be a decisive blow against the forces of capitalism within the Tshwane Metro, which included Babu's Friendly Café on Potgieter Street, which had refused to accept a cadre's job application because Mr. Babu did not recognize a Master's degree earned at the Leonid Brezhnev Technical University of Tractor Maintenance in Minsk.

Pedi said that those living on Fidel Castro Street would "soon come to enjoy the immense benefits" of living in a street modelled after Castro's Cuba.

He confirmed that residents would have free world-class healthcare, excellent medical treatment, top-notch hospital access, superb clinics, highly trained doctors, free world-class healthcare, highly trained doctors, top-notch hospital access, "and lots, lots more".

Asked if residents would have anything other than good healthcare, Pedi said, "No."

"Residents will not be allowed to have newspapers delivered to them, or to watch any television produced outside the Eastern Bloc after 1983," said Pedi.

However, he said, residents would be allowed to take part in an annual May Day parade in which they could celebrate living in "the greatest street in the world".

He said attendance at the parade would not be compulsory, and all those who didn't want to celebrate the life of Castro would be taken by truck to an alternative celebration that involved mining salt.

search results related to: fidel castro street

PETROL PRICE DROPS ALLOW SUV OWNERS TO START ENGINES

JOHANNESBURG. Recent falls in the petrol price have allowed thousands of SUV owners to start their engines after months of being towed around the suburbs by scores of domestic workers in leather harnesses. "I'd forgotten how free you are in a moving SUV," said one driver. "You can drive wherever you want: over traffic islands, across two lanes, whatever."

Her sentiments echoed those of thousands of other luxury vehicle owners whose social schedules had been dictated by the topography of the suburbs.

"I couldn't go to Book Club for five months," said Emily Clutch of Rosebank, Johannesburg, whose domestic worker Beauty Habongwana had refused to tow her BMW X5 to Sandton.

"Luckily all the girls were still there when I went back this week," she said. "In fact they haven't left since August. Maureen Spengler said it was because they all knew once they rolled home they wouldn't be able to go back, so they just stayed.

"They look really bad. Maureen says they've survived on cucumber sandwiches and water from the sprinkler system. And they had to burn the new Patricia Cornwell to stay warm."

Cape Town SUV driver Greta Lebensraum-Fist said she had forgotten how much freedom came with driving.

"I used to love driving my X5, so when it got too expensive I'd sit in the car in the garage and just rock back and forth to get the feeling of going somewhere."

Asked if she had missed the view while sitting in her garage, she said she had not, as she "never looked through the windscreen anyway".

"Everybody knows that you don't look through the windscreen of an X5," she laughed. "You look at the GPS navigation thingy, or you examine the kids in the mirror, to make sure your girl isn't getting fat and that your boy isn't going gay."

Lazanya Mbuli of Houghton said that she experienced "traffic ubuntu" on a daily basis.

"People share with you when you're in an SUV. When the lights are green they tell you by hooting, or when you're accidentally straddling lanes they show you with helpful hand signals.

"I think it's one finger for the left lane and two fingers for the right."

Judi-May Guillotine of Fancourt said she would miss being towed by domestic workers.

"It was so festive, with all their harnesses jingling away in the crisp winter night air, and them all gabbling away to each other in African. I will miss that."

However, she agreed that it was "lovely" to be able to sit once more at green traffic lights and listen to "the little people in their little second-hand cars hoot and hoot and hoot."

search results related to: suv driver

www.hayibo.com

61

ANCYL DEFENDS FUNCTIONAL GRADE WOODWORKER MALEMA

PRETORIA. The ANC Youth League has dismissed evidence of Julius Malema's dismal academic career, saying that the ANCYL is "about the collective and not the individual". However, education officials have confirmed that Malema achieved an H for standard grade Mathematics in matric, suggesting that he probably can't tell the difference between concepts of "one" and "many".

A digital reproduction of Malema's school report card has been circulating in South Africa for some time, revealing a startling array of failing marks, including a G in standard grade Woodworking.

However, the ANCYL has rejected the report, declaring that Malema's mark for Woodwork was a revolutionary rejection of racism.

In a statement released this morning, the League said that one of the founding tenets of racism was that blacks were consigned to being "hewers of wood and carriers of water".

"Woodworking is all about hewing wood and entrenching the hegemony of racism," read the statement. "Comrade Malema was subverting this by failing so selflessly."

It explained that Malema had been planning to construct a baroque cuckoo-clock for his final Grade 12 project, but chose instead to "reject bourgeois values and instead make a dovetail joint, representing the will of the masses".

"However, this plan was betrayed by counterrevolutionary cold-glue which got all over everything, and a racist chisel which split the joint a week before deadline.

"He therefore chose to demonstrate his love for the simple things in life by handing in a sanded plank. This humble gesture of perseverance was rejected by the Apartheid education system, and he was given an H."

Asked how the Apartheid education system was still in control in 2002, the Youth League said that "racism knows no limits" and could "transcend time and space, like a big racist thing in space and time, transcending them, also".

Meanwhile political analysts say they are alarmed by Malema's results in Mathematics.

According to one, who wished to remain anonymous because he wished to remain alive, getting an H on the standard grade meant that Malema was "counting using his fingers and toes, and running into trouble after one hand".

However, most agree that a profoundly limited intellect will not be a hindrance to Malema's political career, as he would only be required to write his own name, usually on blank cheques, spell words like "demand", "reject", "kill" and "enemies", and throw ANC-themes T-shirts into crowds.

"Plus," added the unnamed analyst, "he's got nine more years of school than Jacob Zuma.

"Eleven, if you count the years he repeated."

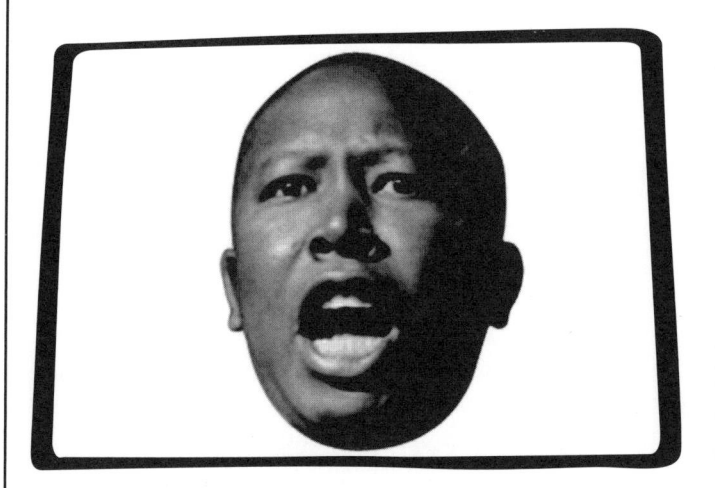

search results related to: malema

BREYTENBACH URGES YOUTH TO FLEE SA, BUT OLD SHOULD STAY AND BE SLAUGHTERED

PARIS. Former literary light and trainee French intellectual Breyten Breytenbach has urged young South Africans to flee the country while they still can. However he offered no advice to older citizens, who should apparently stay behind and be slaughtered until the country is empty and needs to be repopulated with a super-race of Franco-Afrikaner poets.

Breytenbach, who has lived in self-imposed exile in France since the 1960s, wrote his passionate plea to young South Africans in 'Harper's Magazine', a publication that is not read by young South Africans because it is prohibitively expensive and not for sale in South Africa.

In an extract widely quoted in local media he offered what he called "bitter advice".

"If a young South African were to ask me whether he or she should stay or leave, my bitter advice would be to go," writes Breytenbach. It is believed that youth of the country have reacted to the article with some confusion as none of them know who Breytenbach is.

"I thought Breyten Breytenbach was the Latin name for a yeast infection," said Luckystrike Xaba, 18, of Soweto.

"He says, 'If a young South African were to ask me...'," said Chrizanlimarie Brits, 16, of Welkom. "But why would anyone ask him anything when we don't know who he is?" She added that she had been taught not to talk to strangers, especially not strangers "who are from France and have a little bokkie beard like that uncle".

Meanwhile friends and colleagues of Breytenbach have denied that he is militating for a population implosion in South Africa so that he can step in and repopulate the country single-handedly. Jean Frisson, professor of post-literate narrative apologist fetishism in Saharan scourge poetry, conceded that Breytenbach "might have painted himself into a demographical corner".

"Yes, if you urge all the young people to go you're going to be left with a non-breeding population, which will inevitably mean drastic population decline," said Frisson.

"But that doesn't mean Breyten wants to step in and start making babies, however gifted and poetical they might turn out to be."

He also urged young South Africans not to be fearful about employment prospects should they decide to relocate to Europe.

"Clearly it's possible to enjoy a splendid career by settling in Europe and then being paid in dollars for your thoughts on how South Africans should live their lives," he said.

search results related to: breytenbach

ZIMBABWE AIR FORCE BALLOONS SCRAMBLED AHEAD OF BRITISH INVASION

HARARE. Zimbabwe has mobilized its entire air force – three unmanned weather balloons that can be set on fire near enemy aircraft – to meet an expected attack of airborne suicide-homosexuals from the United Kingdom. This morning Robert Mugabe warned Britain that at most three of its bombers would be "severely singed" if they strayed into his airspace.

The mobilization of the ZAF follows weekend revelations from the Zimbabwean Ministry of Information that the non-existent outbreak of cholera currently not ravaging the country was caused by a biochemical attack by Britain.

Addressing journalists from his communications bunker outside Harare this morning, Mugabe said that he had placed the Air Force on high alert after receiving credible intelligence that the Royal Air Force was about to drop suicide-homosexuals on strategic targets across the country.

He reassured the media present that they were safe as the bunker had been reinforced with three Sealy Posturepedic mattresses nationalized from the home of Mrs Jessica Stevens of Jacaranda Crescent, Harare. According to Mugabe the ZAF weather balloon fleet can reach an altitude of 500 meters, which would "render any Royal Air Force incursion as impotent as Tony Blair and his bondage gimp Gordon Brown".

When it was put to him that RAF bombers would probably enter Zimbabwean airspace at about 12,000 metres, Mugabe explained that this was impossible as no human being could survive exposure to the deep cold of outer space, which started at about 600 metres above sea level. He also said that Zimbabwean scientists had proved that Heaven started at 1,000 metres, and that God's kingdom would provide "natural cover" against British air power. "Basically if you fly above 1,000 metres you will explode against Heaven's celestial Vibrocrete wall," explained Mugabe.

However, he conceded that the three flammable weather balloons were probably not an ideal defence against the Royal Air Force, but said that the ZAF's other three aircraft, crop-dusters armed with pesticides that could cause mild skin irritations, were currently not operational after running out of petrol in mid-flight and experiencing "non-scheduled gravity events resulting in flame-related damage".

He would not confirm or deny reports that the ZAF also has one Lear business jet with enough fuel on board for a one-way flight to Switzerland, a hold stocked with tinned food and foreign currency, and a heart-shaped revolving bed under a large poster of the Village People.

www.hayibo.com

300 MINSTRELS IN HOSPITAL AFTER STREET CARNIVAL CRUSHED BY RUSH HOUR TRAFFIC

CAPE TOWN. Over 300 Cape Minstrels are in hospital this morning after taking part in a traditional street carnival to celebrate January 2 without realizing that the day was not a public holiday. According to one Minstrel bandleader, the carnival was "just starting to go lekker" when it was crushed by morning rushhour traffic, scattering Minstrels and crushing ukuleles.

The second day of the year has traditionally been a holiday for many Cape Town citizens, with January 3, 4, 6, 9, 14, 19, and 24 also being viewed as back-up holidays in case the second falls on a weekend. All non-holiday days can also be used for meditation or training in preparation for street carnivals, meaning that most Capetonians work for approximately four hours in January.

However, local government has tried to phase out the holiday, citing lost man-hours and chronic migraines caused by having to listen to plastic ukuleles and discordant brass instruments, and this year January 2 is a normal working day.

The change came as shocking news to the men of the Heppy Cheppie Lekker Larnie Tjakkalang Tjokker Brigade minstrel band who headed this morning's catastrophic carnival.

"Nobody told us it was a working day," said Sexy Boy September, who had eight toes broken by a Volvo.

"They say they faxed us a memo at work, but don't they know we haven't been at work since October?"

According to Clive Cupido of the Dreamlover Waltz and Sokkie Pomp Kings, the carnival was "just starting to go lekker" at around 7am this morning when it moved onto the highway into the city and met with instant carnage.

"I remember we were doing 'My Bonnie Lies over the Ocean', arranged for plastic ukulele and slightly dented harmonica, and suddenly I heard this terrible sound from up at the front of the parade, like a loud metallic grinding and screeching," said Cupido.

"I just thought it was Oompie Avril Daniels warming up his tuba. Now they tell me it was the Nice Naartjie New-Style Jazz Boyz getting ploughed by the 7.03 Golden Arrow bus from Salt River.

"It's not nice to hear that."

Shocked motorists have responded with an outpouring of donations including earplugs, non-sequined clothing, and beginners' guides to music.

"I was looking at my GPS and then I looked up and saw about 5,000 people in sequined boleros and Styrofoam hats right in the middle of the highway," said traumatized driver Margie Kent, who is being investigated for possibly obliterating the Camelot Crooners with her Range Rover.

"In that situation you'd be mad to stop. So I accelerated, and then when I realised I was surrounded I tried to reverse, which probably made it a bit worse."

search results related to: minstrel carnival

HOROSCOPE

Aries Mar 21 - Apr 19

Be especially careful around loved ones who are ill. A repeat of last year's accidental life-support switch-off will not go down well, especially if you again claim you thought it was the plug for the kettle.

www.hayibo.com

FADING MUGABE CONSIDERS EVIL MTV AWARDS COMEBACK

HARARE. Overlooked by Western media and ignored even by his most vociferous critics in South Africa, Zimbabwean despot Robert Mugabe is reportedly eager to emulate Britney Spears by relaunching his career as an international pariah by performing at the MTV Music Video Awards. Mugabe has hinted that he won't sing but instead will do "something really evil".

Aides close to Mugabe say that he has lost much of his old evil vigour in recent months as power-sharing talks in Zimbabwe grind on and the attention of the world's media is drawn by the US elections.

According to court insider Flagellate Chirwa, the President still issues daily press statements denouncing Tony Blair and accusing him of practising homosexual black magic, but with little or no media coverage, he says the old man is fading fast.

"We adore Comrade Mugabe, Liberator of the Masses, Biter of the Ankles of Tony Blair, Castrator of Margaret Thatcher, Seducer of Thabo Mbeki," said Chirwa.

"But even we have to admit that the plots against him are becoming increasingly banal."

He said that last week someone had let all the air out of the tyres of the Presidential bicycle, and Mugabe had issued a statement on national radio accusing the CIA of the attack.

"We later found out it was just a starving Presidential butler from the East Wing of the Grace Mugabe Memorial Pleasure Dome who had been chewing on the wheel," said Chirwa.

However, he said no harm had been done as the radio microphone hadn't been switched on.

"He's been doing off-air broadcasts for a few weeks now," said Chirwa.

"We don't have the heart to tell him there's no electricity, and even if there was, most of the people have eaten their radios."

He said the ongoing publicity slump had also damaged Mugabe's relationship with life partner Thabo Mbeki, and he confirmed that Mugabe and Mbeki were now sleeping in separate bedrooms.

"Thabo says Robert has gone soft and that the spark has gone out of the relationship," said Chirwa.

"Robert never buys him flowers or takes him shopping any more.

"He used to love surprising Thabo with little gifts. Confiscated farms, stuffed ballot boxes, that sort of thing. But not any more. It's really sad."

However, he said, Mugabe was confident that his evil career could be relaunched by a good showing on something like the MTV awards.

"He's always been a fan of Britney," said Chirwa. "In fact 'Hit Me Baby One More Time' is the unofficial anthem of our war veterans."

However, he denied that Mugabe had been seen pouring lighter fluids on large piles of ballot papers from MDC-supporting areas while singing 'Oops! I Did It Again'.

search results related to: international pariah

DEVELOPING WORLD SAVED AS U2 ANNOUNCE NEW ALBUM

ROME. The news that Irish rock group U2 will release a new album in March has been hailed with relief and joy throughout the developing world.

Millions of grateful peasants and refugees mobbed aid workers in Africa and Asia, offering sacrifices of new crops and young lambs to lead singer Bono for gracing the world with yet another insight into poverty.

The band made the announcement this morning from the Pope's private balcony overlooking St Peter's Square in the Vatican, while a text version was transmitted simultaneously to non-governmental aid missions around the world.

According to Vatican insiders, the Pope had been asked to surrender his private rooms to accommodate Bono, and had gratefully accepted, leaving a glass of milk and some cookies next to the microphone.

Meanwhile UNICEF spokesman Pierre Saboteur said that the announcement was a "Christmas and New Year miracle for the squalid, the oppressed, the filthy and downtrodden".

He would not be drawn on whether this group included young South African graduates living in London.

"For years we have been praying to our respective gods, all over the world, to inspire Bono with divine wisdom so that he might compose some more rousing riffs for The Edge to play, to help us all understand the plight of the needy," said Saboteur.

"This is an answer to those prayers."

He said that aid workers in South-East Asia had reported a surge in charitable donations from starving peasants in recent weeks, as tens of millions offered lambs, bushels of corn and IOUs for future earnings at temples and mosques across the region in the hope that they might expedite the release of the new album.

The news also prompted fresh celebration of Bono's net worth, which is estimated to be about $500 million, an amount that inspires and reassures billions of malnourished children around the planet.

"Sometimes when I am chewing my daily rice grain I feel sad," said Joseph Kibuki, 9, of Burundi.

"But then they tell me Mr Bono is so rich, and I know that there is a God and that good people are rewarded.

"Or at least cool people."

"Perhaps one day Mr Bono will come to my country and shine his holy light onto me. And he will bring running water. And pretty back-up singers wearing ethically made T-shirts highlighting my plight on television, between 'The Apprentice' and reruns of 'The Golden Girls'." ★

search results related to: bono's holy light

HOROSCOPE

Capricorn Dec 22 - Jan 19

This week you will yearn for the country life. Until you drive into the country and remember that it's full of shops without fridges selling lukewarm 7-Up and garlic polony.

OBAMA '08: ZILLE TOLD SHE'S NOT PRESIDENT OF US

CAPE TOWN. Democratic Alliance leader Helen Zille is reportedly "gutted" after briefly believing that she had been elected as the 44th President of the United States. Ms Zille was reportedly woken at 5am this morning by a screaming aide who told her that "the leader of the Democratic Party" had taken the White House, and, she said, she made a "faulty assumption".

Zille could not be contacted for much of the morning, as she had spent the early hours getting her hair bronzed into its trademark helmet form and had been meeting with interior decorators for advice on how to turn the White House into a less austere family home.

After realizing that she had in fact not been elected President of the United States, she then had to spend several hours doing damage control, which included trying to get a refund for four million red, white and blue balloons.

However, she confirmed that the party would be unable to recoup a large deposit paid for a minibus with loudspeakers mounted on the roof that was going to drive through the Southern Suburbs playing a selection of Ms Zille's favourite American music, including excerpts by Jive Bunny and the Mastermixers and Tupac Shakur's greatest hits performed by the Mormon Tabernacle Choir.

When she finally appeared to brief the press, trailing a half-deflated red balloon behind her, a visibly emotional Zille congratulated Barack Obama on his win.

"This is a good day for America," she said.

"It could have been a better day. I'm not bitter. I'm just saying. But it's still an okay day.

"I mean, it could have been an awesome day. But they blew it."

Asked what her next move would be, Zille said she would wait for her hair to rust into a more manageable shape, and then "start the slow, painful climb back towards some sort of meaning in this depressing cul-de-sac of a country, a million light years from the centre of power, that glittering city on a hill that is Washington, where dreams become reality and joy trickles out of the taps".

She confirmed that after the press conference she would be addressing a row in the Cape Town City Council, with rival factions each accusing the other of "not being lekker" on a variety of issues including the ongoing pigeon dung crisis and new legislation allowing council workers to sleep face-down on any stretch of municipal grass, any time during office hours.

search results related to: bursting zille's balloons

OTHER BREAKING NEWS

★ **Zille paralyses face with Botox to reflect paralysed party**

★ **Mandela urges Obama to go to jail for 27 years to boost image**

★ **Sol Kerzner challenges New Jersey mafia to kitsch-off**

★ **US reveals reason for ongoing support of Israel is Ark of Covenant**

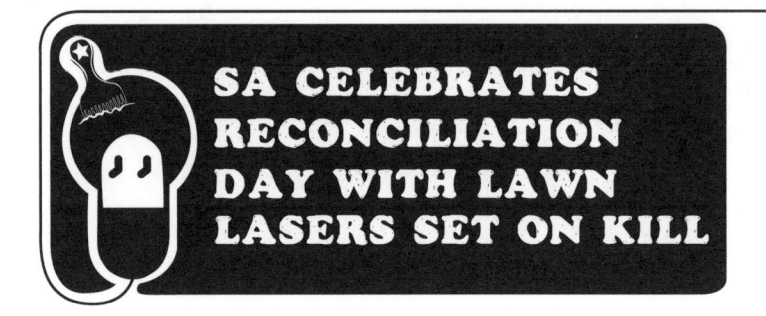

SA CELEBRATES RECONCILIATION DAY WITH LAWN LASERS SET ON KILL

JOHANNESBURG. After centuries of being kept apart by racist policies and brutal security forces, South Africans have celebrated the Day of Reconciliation at home, kept apart by racist Dobermans and brutal armed response companies. According to a poll, most have set their lawn lasers on kill, locked their doors, and will spend the day watching 'WWE Smackdown'.

The Day of Reconciliation was introduced in 1994 after decades in which December 16 had been observed as a religious holiday by the apartheid regime, commemorating the day on which a small band of settlers, armed only with rifles and 13 million rounds of ammunition, fought off a host of Zulu warriors armed with pointy sticks.

The holiday came to be known as the Day of the Vow, although many white South Africans continued to refer to it throughout the 1950s as Eat Hot Lead You Zulu Freaks Day, or simply as Nya Nya Nya Nyaaa Nyaaaa Day.

The origins of the Day of the Vow have also been questioned by new research which shows that another Day of the Vow was observed at the Cape between 1654 and 1659, after Dutch founder Jan van Riebeeck tested negative for gonorrhoea and pubic lice and vowed never to frequent Vrot Magda's Hoer Emporium in Buitenkant Street ever again.

However, the advent of a democratic government in 1994 saw the holiday replaced with the Day of Reconciliation, which hoped to bring the country's races closer together and to instil a sense of common destiny.

According to a poll conducted this morning, most people said they wanted to embrace their identity as citizens of the new South Africa, and would therefore spend the day locked inside their houses with either a gun or a panic button on the couch next to them, watching 'WWE Smackdown'.

Asked if they would be reaching out and reconciling with citizens of other race groups, black respondents said that they would probably not, as it was difficult to make themselves heard over the baying of Dobermans, the wailing of alarms, and sporadic gunfire from the machine-gun nest in the granny flat.

For their part whites said that they would not be reaching out to blacks as they didn't know which blacks to reach out to.

"I'd love to reconcile with them," said respondent Gloria Braak. "But there's ten blacks for every white. That means nine blacks are going to feel really left out.

"That's not very reconciliatory. It's much less hurtful to just stay at home and warn the kids not to accidentally touch the electrified Trellidor."

search results related to: lawn laser

FANCOURT RESIDENTS IN SHOCK AFTER SEEING BLACK PEOPLE, OLD CARS

GEORGE. Up to fifty residents of the luxury Fancourt golf estate are being treated for severe shock after their tour bus accidentally left the estate and wandered into nearby George. According to medical staff, the victims were severely traumatized by seeing black people who weren't gardeners or maids, and being exposed to compact two-year-old cars.

The tour bus had been scheduled to take the residents from the Gary Player Ubuntu Activity Centre down to the Cecil John Rhodes Imperial Chapel for a motivational lecture on conforming. However, according to shocked survivors the driver had suddenly exited the Ossewa-Brandwag Memorial Gate and they had found themselves "in hell".

"Everyone started screaming and clawing at the windows," recalled survivor Grietjie van Pond, 56. "When you move into Fancourt they make you swear on a copy of Paulo Coelho's 'The Alchemist' that you will never leave the estate, for your own protection, so we knew we were in terrible danger."

Another victim, who surrendered both her names when she got married and is now simply known as Mrs Brad Roberts, told journalists that they had immediately seen black people walking in the street, and had asked the panicked driver why the black people were not wearing regulation overalls or riding mowers.

"He said they had been emancipated. I just vomited on the window with shock," she said.

Lymphoma Swanepoel, 44, said she had felt "sick and dizzy" when they stopped at a red light and a young black man looked directly at her.

"I'll never forget it until the day they scatter my ashes on the Ernie Els Woodland Water Feature down by the 16th fairway," she said.

"He looked straight at me, in my eyes, and said 'Howzit'.

"Not 'Hau, miesies, hoe gaan dit?' or 'Molo, meddem'.

"He didn't even ask me how the kleinbaas and kleinmiesies were doing at school, or say that he was too much happy that they were well. It was obscene."

It is also believed that many of the victims saw cars that were older than a year and were not Range Rovers. However, trauma counsellors say the victims are too distressed at the moment to describe their encounter with what may have been a two-year-old hatchback Volkswagen.

According to trauma counsellor Huggies Msimang, many of the victims were finding it impossible to deal with seeing a new reality.

"When you live in a fake house in a fake landscape, paid for with fake money earned in fake business dealings, black people and small Volkwagens can be deeply frightening," she said. ✪

search results related to: white luxury

ULTRA-FERTILE ANGELINA CONCEIVES AT BAFTAS, HOPES TO GIVE BIRTH LIVE AT OSCARS

LONDON. Ultra-fertile Hollywood couple Angelina Jolie and Brad Pitt have announced that they are expecting octuplets after accidentally conceiving during the Bafta Awards in London on the weekend. The couple say they are hoping to deliver the babies live on international television at the Academy Awards later this month after a pregnancy of just three weeks.

Addressing the media this morning, a spokesman for the couple confirmed that octuplets had been conceived at the Bafta Awards when Jolie had paused to adjust her dress on the red carpet and Pitt had accidentally walked into her.

"It's the risk you take when you're the two most fertile people in the world," said spokesman Larry Katzenjammer. "Having said that, the eight lives that spring from this fleeting union will of course be treasured, especially by glossy society magazines."

He said that Jolie and Pitt had decided to try to give birth at the Oscars.

"They know it'll be tough because the Oscars are only three weeks away," said Katzenjammer. "But the more kids Angie has, the more time she's shaving off the whole pregnancy process. She's like a machine."

Both stars have been nominated at this year's Academy Awards, with Jolie tipped as a clear winner in the category Best Portrayal of a Real Actress by an Inflatable Lip, while Pitt is to receive a Lifetime Achievement Award for having recently added a third facial expression to his acting repertoire.

Pitt said that he was delighted to be an expectant father again but expressed relief that their union had only been a slight collision and not a more violent impact or his virility might have "caused a real problem come Oscar night".

"The Academy has a very tight schedule," said Katzenjammer. "Brad is just so thankful that they're only going to have eight kids that night, because it would be really awkward if the orchestra started trying to get Angie off the stage while she was delivering their tenth or fifteenth baby of the evening."

Asked how many children the couple were planning to have, Katzenjammer said that they were hoping for "anything between 100 and 300".

"This year," he added. "Obviously 2010 is another year, and I think they're looking at maybe another 200 or so.

"Maybe more if Angie keeps making forgettable movies." ✪

ELECTION SCHEDULED FOR APRIL 22, GRANDIOSE CLAIMS SCHEDULED FOR APRIL 21

PRETORIA. Political parties in South Africa have welcomed the announcement of this year's election date and have promised to have their rhetoric in top gear by then. Political analysts have tipped the ANC to produce the most grandiose claims before April 22, but they agree the Democratic Alliance can score an upset with some wild last-minute claims.

President Kgalema Motlanthe took time off from his busy schedule of being invisible to announce the election date, confirming that April 21 will be the day on which grandiose claims by competing parties reach a climax.

ANC spokesman Screamer Mkhize said his organization was confident of an overwhelming victory in the rhetorical battle that lay ahead, thanks to a long tradition of flowery rhetoric.

"Disciplined cadres can speak uninterrupted for up to nine minutes without drawing breath," said Mkhize.

"If we sense that we are about to be interrupted by a counterrevolutionary, we simply repeat a word so they can't interject.

"The result is that we we we we we we we we we we we can eh eh eh eh eh eh eh eh eh eh claim most of the the the the the the the the the the the airtime just by sounding eh eh eh eh eh eh eh eh eh eh as if we are eh eh eh eh eh eh eh eh choosing our words very carefully."

He said the ANC has been resting Youth League President and rhetorical savant Julius Malema so that he can be on top form by the week of the election.

He said he had no idea what Malema would say on April 21, as he wrote his own scripts, usually in crayon on his playroom wall.

Malema was not available for comment as he was taking part in a break-dancing competition next to the swings, but insiders believe he will claim that the ANC is the greatest party in the history of the universe, and that if it ever came down to a fight between the ANC, the ancient Romans and the British Navy of the 1940s, the ANC would win without breaking a sweat.

Meanwhile the Democratic Alliance has vowed to up the rhetorical ante by trying to make claims that are not direct attacks on the ANC.

Spokesman Worsie Verwoerd said that the party had decided to be much less negative and more forward-looking.

"We've realised that we can't just have a platform where all we do is criticize the ANC," he said. "We've got to stand for something, not just against the ANC.

"Which is why we in the Not-ANC are looking forward, and therefore away from the ANC, to a not-ANC future in which our non-ANC Youth League children can not vote ANC and get jobs not supplied by the ANC."

He added that the DA boasted numerous achievements that could not be matched by any other party.

"For example, out of all the party leaders who are white women called Helen, we've got the best one," he said.

"Plus nobody else has a better red, white and blue logo, prominently featuring the letters D and A. We've really set the bar very high there." ✪

SURVEY

Jacob Zuma's first act as president of South Africa in 2009 should be to:

○ Smear himself with Vaseline and squeeze through the window of his cell

○ Dip Helen Zille in honey and throw her to the lesbians

○ Invade Lesotho as a warning to the Democratic Alliance

○ Have Thabo Mbeki stuffed and mounted above the fireplace at Nkandla, next to his stuffed copy of the constitution

○ Ask FIFA to give the World Cup back to South Africa. Bribe them if necessary with used corvettes and never-used submarines

MANDELA URGES OBAMA TO GO TO JAIL FOR 27 YEARS TO BOOST IMAGE

PRETORIA. International icon Nelson Mandela has hailed Barack Obama's historic victory but has cautioned that if Obama wants to be remembered as a giant of history he will also need to be jailed for 27 years by athletic white supremacists. Obama has reportedly heeded the call and is trying to negotiate a part-time 27-year sentence with prison authorities in Australia.

Speaking to the press via telephone from inside his cryogenics tank, Mandela said that Obama would have to make sacrifices if his legacy was to endure.

"Many people ask me why I gave up 27 years of my life in order to revive the musical career of Bob Geldof," said Mandela.

"The answer is simple. I would do it again in a heartbeat. A talent like Geldof and the Boomtown Rats is something that must be treasured. It is greater than one human life."

He added that the same would apply to Bono if the Irishman's popularity ever waned.

"If people stopped buying his albums, perhaps because they realised that all his songs are just one note, sort of yodelled, I would report to the nearest police station at once," said Mandela.

However, he added that this was unlikely as Bono had "got himself a very good gig riding the war, poverty and famine wave, which is lovely job security".

Mandela said that Obama had the potential to be remembered as one of the greatest statesmen the world has ever known, and if he was lucky he might also one day be allowed to make short statements about global issues at a Bob Geldof or Bono concert.

But, he said, before that could happen Obama would need to be jailed for 27 years by rugby-loving sunshine-worshipping white supremacists.

The American President-elect has reportedly taken the warning to heart, with an aide confirming this morning that Obama is trying to negotiate a part-time 27-year-sentence with prison authorities in Perth, Australia.

"First prize was obviously Robben Island," said the aide.

"But we did the research and it turns out most of the whites that supported apartheid and wanted Madiba locked away now live in Perth, so it looks like it will work out after all."

Meanwhile Australian authorities have denied being white supremacists, adding that many of their best friends know a black person.

search results related to: robben island

HOROSCOPE

Virgo Aug 23 - Sep 22

Your bad sex life is directly related to work stress. Get to the root of the problem. Have sex with your boss.

BOKS TO SALUTE MAMA AFRICA WITH CLICK SONG

LONDON. The Springbok rugby team has confirmed that it will honour South African musical icon Miriam Makeba by performing her trademark 'click song' instead of the national anthem ahead of Saturday's test against England. According to a spokesman, the thirteen players who had failed to master the clicks would snap their fingers at appropriate moments.

Speaking to journalists this morning outside the team's Brixton hotel, spokesman Curly Zinza said that the Springboks had been unanimous in their wish to honour the late singer known as Mama Africa.

"Most of the guys thought 'Nkosi Sikelel' iAfrika' was the Click Song, so it wasn't much of a leap," said Zinza.

However, he said, despite a week of intensive rehearsal with the South London Jubilation and Vengeance Baptist Ladies' Tenor Choir, most of the squad had been unable to master the many clicking sounds in the song.

"Only three of the guys managed it," said Zinza, declining to name them in case they were targeted by Saru management for being militant Africanists.

He said that two of the three players were white and were so excited at being able to say the various clicks that they were now inserting them wherever they could.

"It's not a major problem but we did have to explain to the guys that it's 'Nkosi Sikelel' iAfrika', not 'Xosi Sixelel' iAfrixa'," said Zinza.

He confirmed that the rest of the squad would snap their fingers in tune to the music.

Controversial loose-forward Luke Watson, who ruled himself out of the tour citing chronic nausea, is said to be devastated by the decision to replace the anthems with Makeba's classic tune.

"Obviously Luke feels pretty sick about it," said Zinza.

"He's been practising his clicks for years, and to miss out on a chance to showcase his struggle credentials is really hard on him."

Meanwhile Bakkies Botha is reportedly recovering well after collapsing earlier in the week when he was told that Mama Africa had passed away.

"Bakkies took the news incredibly hard," said Zinza, adding that the giant lock had fainted in their hotel's lobby, crushing to death five Japanese tourists who had wandered too close.

However, he said Botha's condition had improved rapidly once he had been told that it was Makeba who had died and not Sonja Herholdt.

search results related to: bakkies fainting

RALPH FIENNES TO PLAY LEON SCHUSTER IN ART-HOUSE BIOPIC

JOHANNESBURG. As Leon Schuster's 'Mister Bones 2' opens nationwide, art-house filmmakers Merchant Ivory have confirmed that the comedian is to be the subject of a new biopic that will celebrate how he built an empire on saying "Hau!", wove narratives around diarrhoea and perfected a brand of humour that contains no humour. Ralph Fiennes is tipped to play Schuster.

Schuster is the highest-grossing filmmaker in South Africa, a nation in which 'Vetkoek Paleis' remains the top-rated sitcom of all time and which has consistently voted for the same politicians despite being ignored by them since 1994.

However, this morning a spokesman for Merchant Ivory, Rupert Thrust, said that those who believed Schuster was trading on an unsophisticated audience were missing the bigger picture.

"Like Fellini or Bergman, Schuster captures a mood," said Thrust.

"The way he frames mobile toilets toppling over to reveal a tourist tormented by diarrhoea he got thanks to being fed a bottle of laxatives by a cheeky black dwarf, it's just breathtaking."

He said that Schuster had deconstructed the concept of excrement and had reinvented it for the post-slapstick audience of the 21st century.

"Somehow he gets inside the mind of the poo. He thinks like the poo. He becomes the poo.

"I don't think it's an exaggeration to say that Schuster's films are literally poo."

He said that the film would foreground the "Kafka-esque despair" that Schuster highlights in each of his features.

"They're marketed as comedies, but when you leave a Schuster film you are overwhelmed with despair," he said. "It's a sobering wake-up call about the world in which we live, and the depths to which we've sunk as a species."

Meanwhile actor Ralph Fiennes has admitted that he is feeling the pressure of playing Schuster, and says he is spending up to six hours a day with a personal trainer, trying to perfect his timing in numerous stunts involving throwing poo at wild animals.

"There's also an incredibly difficult routine where a fat woman falls on my face, and my legs kick out and knock over a portable toilet, and the villain who has diarrhoea and is Superglued to the seat get a fright and runs with the toilet attached to his buttocks into a thorn bush where a monkey throws poo into his mouth.

"They just don't write stuff like this anymore," he said.

search results related to: toilet humour

OTHER BREAKING NEWS

★ **Light drinking no risk but babies urged to avoid binge drinking**

★ **Report says obesity deadlier than terrorism, US mulls bombing fat people**

★ **Patricia de Lille vows to fight screechiness in her voice**

KURT DARREN 46664 SHAME STUNS WORLD

LONDON. The performance of South African pop singer Kurt Darren in Saturday's 46664 concert in Hyde Park, and his subsequent shaming by reggae legend Eddy Grant, has left millions of South Africans stunned and traumatized. Human rights experts said it would take time to "figure out which was worse: the performance, or the shaming that followed it".

Tens of thousands of spectators in Hyde Park and a television audience of almost a billion watched as Darren joined Grant in a rendition of Grant's anti-apartheid anthem, 'Give Me Hope Joanna'.

But according to stunned witnesses, interest turned to horror as Darren seemed to try to affect a West Indian accent, a move described by human rights experts as "unwise".

"Even people who are good at accents don't always get them right on the night," said Advocate Etienne Lafayette of The Hague's International Criminal Court, which is considering investigating the reason for the duet.

"But what happened to Mr Darren was unfortunate."

He said investigators were still trying to establish whether the accent Darren had attempted had been a Caribbean lilt, "or just Pretoria English gone tragically wrong".

However, according to trauma counsellors, who were inundated with calls after the concert, the shock of the performance paled next to the atrocity committed by Grant once the song had ended.

"We can only assume that Mr Grant felt that Mr Darren had been overshadowed, or had perhaps been overwhelmed by the occasion," said Lafayette.

"Perhaps he realised that the cameras had been following him and ignoring Mr Darren. Perhaps he simply looked at Mr Darren and took pity on what he saw."

Pointing to Darren as the South African skulked at the back of the stage, Grant told one sixth of the world's population that Darren had "come all the way from South Africa" and that he was "really popular there".

According to Lafayette, few civilians could recover from this intensity of embarrassment.

"I'm sure Mr Darren is his own harshest critic, which means he was probably flagellating himself after the show; but for Grant to have to resort to telling the audience that he 'is really popular there' was simply excruciating, both for Darren and for all South Africans."

Meanwhile concert organizers have brushed off the incident, insisting that the 46664 event had achieved its intended purpose.

"The 46664 celebration has three primary goals," said organizer Sybil Thring.

"Firstly, and most obviously, to exploit Nelson Mandela while we still can.

"Secondly, to prop up the flagging careers of ageing British rock stars.

"And thirdly, to make middle-class British people and white South African expats feel really good about themselves.

"I think we nailed all three."

OTHER BREAKING NEWS

★ **Paris Hilton enters climate change debate, accepts blame for 'global hotness'**

★ **German leader apologizes for 80s pop duo atrocity**

★ **Man admits he is one of 18 South Africans who haven't read 'Spud'**

SA POST OFFICE TO SELL STOLEN AMAZON PRODUCTS DIRECT TO PUBLIC

PRETORIA. A day after US online retail giant Amazon announced that it was no longer offering South African customers standard postal delivery due to massive theft by SA Post Office employees, the Post Office has announced that it will sell cut-price books, DVDs and CDs direct to the public outside the back door of its branches nationwide.

According to a statement made by Post Office spokesman Gift Mkhize, the new retail outlets would operate on a cash-only, first-come first-served, don't-ask-don't-tell basis.

He added that for those customers who did not feel like queuing there would be "mobile franchises" parked near most branches, where the public was welcome to buy goods out of the boots of Post Office employees' cars.

Asked if the Post Office was ashamed at being the only postal service in Africa to be blacklisted by the US retail giant, Mkhize was defiant, saying that Amazon's bold branding on its packaging was to blame for the rampant pilfering.

"Those parcels have 'Amazon' written all over them," he said. "Our employees find this very provocative.

"Most of our staff are functionally illiterate, but over the years, handling many printed items, some of them have developed a rudimentary sense of lettering, and that big A and big Z are unmistakable."

He said that expecting Post Office staff not to pocket their clients' packages was "as naïve as expecting Members of Parliament not to fiddle their expense accounts".

According to Mkhize, the decision to sell merchandise outside the back door of branches had been made at board level, after initial anti-theft measures proved ineffective.

He said that a 2003 initiative to install metal detectors at staff entrances had been compromised when all the metal detectors were stolen by employees, who then sold them back to the Post Office, which subsequently lost them.

"It was very demoralizing," he said. "At least this way our employees feel like stakeholders in the whole process."

Meanwhile a police spokesman has admitted that postal theft is very difficult to tackle.

Superintendent Magda Siff said that the problem was compounded by the fact that Post Offices clerks traditionally moved "incredibly slowly".

"Anyone who has ever used a Post Office in South Africa knows that it takes up to twenty minutes for the sullen lady at Counter 4 to get off her stool, waddle into a back room, have a cup of tea and packet of Tennis biscuits, and waddle back with the wrong parcel.

"During this time she has any number of opportunities to secrete away DVDs and suchlike in her industrial-strength underwear."

She said new bras featuring heavy-duty underwires, high-tensile nylon straps and titanium clasps could cope with much greater loads.

"We're seeing small TVs, ant farms, box sets of 'Desperate Housewives'. That kind of stuff."

She urged the public to report suspiciously rectangular breasts by calling the police's postal theft hotline at 1-800-LOS-DAAI-DOOS.

search results related to: sa post office delivery

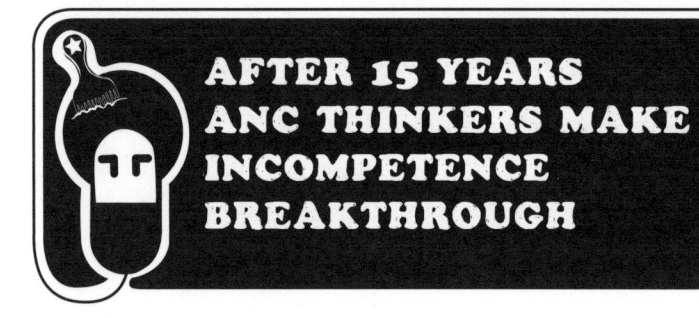

AFTER 15 YEARS ANC THINKERS MAKE INCOMPETENCE BREAKTHROUGH

PRETORIA. After fifteen years in power the ANC has for the first time threatened to sack non-performing ministers, saying that the groundbreaking concept to stop rewarding incompetence went against everything the new South Africa stood for but was necessary if the ruling party was going to carry out effective purges inside its organization.

Speaking to journalists this morning, ANC spokesman Yesman Mxenge said that the new concept, called "accountability", had sown panic and confusion among ANC backbenchers.

"The problem is that it's a very high-end concept," said Mxenge. "I'm not sure I understand it myself.

"In a nutshell, it's basically that if you don't do the job you're being paid half a million a year to do, you don't get fired.

"Wait, no, you do get fired. That's the part that keeps tripping us up."

Asked if the new concept had been inspired by discontent from the electorate, Mxenge said that while voters' opinions were very important they were not very important at all.

"It's a two-way relationship," he said. "The masses put us here, and we keep the masses there. We're happy with that relationship, and I'm sure they are too."

He added that the masses "don't really seem to care" whether ANC politicians were competent or not.

"We've won a bigger majority in every election we've contested, despite doubling the number of hours our backbenchers sleep in their offices every year, and quadrupling the catering budget."

He said the dramatic breakthrough had come unexpectedly at a meeting of senior party leadership where Jacob Zuma was reading through a list of his enemies in the party and "wondering aloud how he could purge them from the ANC without frightening white business".

"Just then Comrade Julius Malema redeployed himself from his playroom into the meeting, pushing one of his toy fire-engines in front of him and making siren sounds, and suggested that they set enemies on fire so that he could put them out with his fire-engine."

He said they had discussed the possibility of incinerating opponents but had ultimately decided against it, as there would be significant legal costs involved, as well as a carbon footprint.

"That's when they came up with firing," said Mxenge. "It goes counter to everything this country stands for, just firing incompetent people without offering them two years of paid leave, but the purge can't wait.

"People. I meant people. Not the purge. The people can't wait." ✪

J&B MET ORGANIZERS CONFIRM PUTTING MODELS TO SLEEP AFTER BROKEN LEGS

CAPE TOWN. Organisers of the prestigious J&B Met horse race have confirmed that two models had to be humanely euthanased after breaking their legs at the gala event on the weekend. According to a spokesman, the models had fallen after becoming drunk and toppling off their stiletto heels, and had been led around the back, given a sugar cube, and put to sleep.

The incident occurred just before the Juvenile Sweepstakes in which breeder Percy Sledge was forced to accept paternity of a teenage son.

According to a spokesman for the organizers, the two models had wandered away from their trainer and had become frightened by the noise of a passing helicopter.

"Models are herd animals and can get very skittish if exposed to unfamiliar sounds such as helicopters, loud bangs, and Bach cantatas," said the spokesman.

"Like all the models, these two had been drinking heavily since dawn, trying to dull the pain of their meaningless existence, and despite having worn six-inch heels since they were ten years old, they both lost control of their footwear and fell.

"As everybody in the horseracing industry knows, a model with a broken leg cannot be rehabilitated, and so they were removed by our on-site veterinarian and humanely euthanased around the back of the beer tent."

The models' trainer and manager, legendary model trainer Miguel "Fingers" De Silva, said he was devastated by the loss.

"You invest so much in taming and raising these girls," said De Silva, recalling how he had found the models as teenagers running wild in the cafés of Camps Bay in Cape Town.

"So much work. Getting close enough to get a rope around their necks; breaking them in my model paddock; teaching them to let a stylist close to them; winning their trust with sugar cubes and expensive drugs. So much work."

Asked how a fall could break their legs, De Silva blamed low bone density caused by chronic malnutrition.

"The really top girls, the ones we breed for these kinds of events, their bones are like glass. They haven't had calcium since they were breastfeeding, and that wasn't for long because their mothers were models too who found the whole thing really gross and stopped as soon as they could."

He said the two models in question had had a problem with alcohol.

"I teach my girls to hold their liquor. I tell them, 'Girls, this martini is all you're going to put into your stomach today, so make it last.' That way they don't wolf it down or throw it up."

But, he said, the two deceased models had always resisted his regimen of alcohol, preferring hard drugs and orange juice instead.

"They just didn't have a tolerance like my other girls," said De Silva. "I feel I am to blame. I should have been there for them. Or at least forced vodka down their throats every other day." ✪

search results related to: broken model

SOUTH AFRICANS, SICK AND TIRED OF BENNI MCCARTHY, THREATEN VIOLENCE

JOHANNESBURG. South Africans have sent a strong message to their country's media, telling them to stop writing and broadcasting stories about erratic football star Benni McCarthy or to face being petrol-bombed. McCarthy, already considered passé by the late 1990s, has once again been in the headlines this week, triggering a potential wave of anti-football hooliganism.

In a strongly worded letter sent to news-desks around the country, Basil Coetzee of People Against News About Benni said his organization had been given a mandate by South Africans to stamp out reportage about "one of the most pointless, dull and depressing pseudo-celebrities ever produced by this country".

According to Coetzee, PANAB has received 9.3 million letters and emails since McCarthy returned to front pages and lamppost placards around the country last week, all calling for drastic action to be taken to silence the endless coverage of someone he describes as "the poster-boy for the zero-charisma set".

"Let me be very clear about this," Coetzee said. "If we read one more story about Benni squabbling with local soccer bosses, or Benni the wasted talent, or Benni's club schedule clashing with national commitments, or in fact anything to do with Benni – his favourite colour, the puppy he had when he was 7 – there's going to be blood."

PANAB was recently placed on the United States' watch list of organizations considered potential terrorist threats, but Coetzee reassured the US State Department that Americans had nothing to fear.

"As long as they don't give Benni a contract with L.A. Galaxy and start giving him column inches in the 'L.A. Times', our cadres will not act against them."

He would not elaborate further on who PANAB's cadres were, but he hinted that there were "at least seven English department academics and some nuns" who could be called upon at any time. He said they were "willing to go to extremes" to enforce a media blackout of McCarthy.

"They have all personally promised me that they are ready to lay down their lives for our struggle," said Coetzee. "Or at least write some very angry letters to the University newspaper, and give their colleagues disparaging looks when they open a newspaper on the sports pages." ✪

GUTTED RHEMA LEADER NOT ALLOWED TO WRESTLE JACOB ZUMA

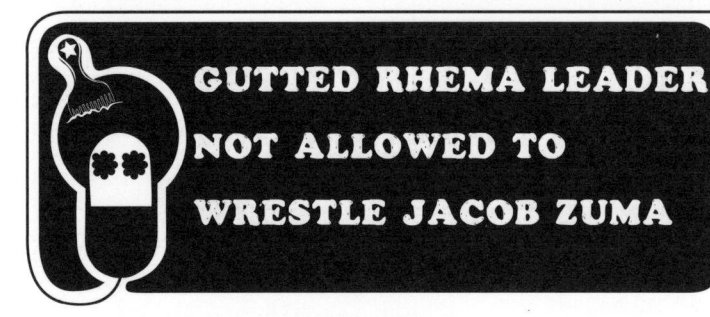

JOHANNESBURG. Church leader Ray McCauley says he is devastated at not being allowed to wrestle ANC President Jacob Zuma during a campaign speech at his church on the weekend. According to McCauley's aides, he had thought Zuma had come to create a biblical tableau in which Jacob wrestles an angel. "He assumed he was the angel," said an aide. "He's gutted."

McCauley, a former bodybuilder, had reportedly been working on a series of biblically inspired wrestling grips in the mistaken belief that Zuma was coming to the Rhema church to wrestle rather than address his congregation.

"Pastor Ray just assumed there would be hand-to-hand combat," explained Rhema spokesman Herod Nyamende.

"Nobody thought Mr Zuma would be stupid enough to come here and campaign. I mean, can you say 'godless communists'?

"We can. In fact, we do. Very often."

He said that the "only logical conclusion left" had been that Zuma had come for a decisive showdown with McCauley to "re-enact Jacob's fight with the angel in Genesis 32, to prove which of them is a bigger stud".

"Pastor Ray was really psyched," said Nyamende. "He's been working on a killer series of moves.

"First he was going to go with And I Shall Smite Thee, which is a forceful laying of hands on the back of the neck, kind of in a chopping motion.

"Then he follows it up with Samson's Ass, where you grab your opponent's jawbone and try to pull it off. If that doesn't work then he slips into Way Down in Egypt Land, where you reach into his underpants with righteous vengeance, grab and twist.

"It was going to be awesome, and obviously Pastor Ray is gutted."

Meanwhile the ANC has apologized for the confusion, but added that McCauley's dreams of wrestling Zuma were "naïve".

"Pastor Ray is a fine man, mainly because he can bench-press more than any other religious leader in the world, including the Pope who can bench about 250 kilograms," said ANC spokesman Kickbax Tswele.

"But he is dreaming if he thinks he can wrestle Comrade Zuma successfully.

"There is no human being alive today who can pin down Comrade Zuma. Whatever you throw at him, he will wriggle free."

search results related to: ray mccauley vs zuma

MUGABE TO APPOINT NEW WAR VETERANS AS REAL ONES ARE ALL DEAD

HARARE. Zimbabwean despot Robert Mugabe will confer official war veteran status on 500,000 teenage boys this weekend as part of his 85th birthday celebrations, after it emerged that the last genuine veteran of the liberation war died of cholera this morning. The new war veterans will be tasked with "rebuilding Zimbabwe by hitting MDC pigs with half-bricks".

The current life expectancy in Zimbabwe is 41, and given that the country's liberation war ended in 1980, the only surviving genuine veterans would had to have enlisted at the age of 12.

According to the country's national archives, currently housed in a chest freezer in a field outside Harare, the youngest recruit was Twinkie Matumbara, 13, who was sold to the Zanu armed forced by his parents who wanted their son to see the world and thought the militia was a travelling circus.

Matumbara reportedly passed away in 2006 after choking on a mouse he had caught and boiled, his first solid food in more than four months.

78

However, other veterans were luckier. Field Marshal Brooklax Chaturanga, who commanded the 14th Light Mounted Poltroons between 1978 and 1980, had just celebrated his 104th birthday last month when a family member stepped on his oxygen tube and he passed away.

In a small ceremony, at which packs of feral dogs were shooed away from the gravesite and vultures were kept at bay with parasols, well-wishers remembered a hero and patriot who attributed his long life to clean living, dedication to his country, and having all of his medical expenses since 1994 paid by South African taxpayers.

Chaturanga was believed to have been the last surviving genuine veteran, but new evidence emerged this week that Banjo Hungwe, 48, had once thrown a spade at colonial forces, making him officially the only veteran still alive.

However, two days after the discovery Hungwe contracted cholera and passed away.

A saddened Mugabe said this morning that his veterans would be sorely missed, especially now that he would have to stop eating nightingale tongues long enough to go out and find some more people who could hit his opponents with half-bricks.

"The war is over but the battle continues," said Mugabe, dabbing merlot off his chin. "The British homosexuals are everywhere. And as Zimbabwean science has shown, there is only one cure for Britishness and homosexuality: a half-brick to the face."

He said he had tasked his aides with finding 500,000 teenage boys who would be given official war veteran status and who could be "handed the half-brick of destiny, to totally mash up the heads of the imperialist dogs".

However, aides who did not wish to be named confirmed this morning that they are struggling to find 500,000 teenage boys healthy enough to pick up a half-brick.

"All the ones who are strong enough to walk or crawl are in South Africa," said one.

"It's very disappointing that they can't make an effort for the man who has saved Zimbabwe. We just hope it doesn't spoil Comrade Mugabe's birthday.

"People can be so selfish." ✪

ZIMBABWE TO CURE CHOLERA EPIDEMIC WITH SALMA HAYEK BREAST MILK

HARARE. Zimbabwe's Health Minister, Tampax Watmiwari, has vowed to end the cholera epidemic in his country by introducing Mexican actress Salma Hayek's breast milk into Zimbabwe's water supply. According to extensive research conducted by the Ministry outside the Bulawayo Shoprite, only Hayek can save Zimbabwe as she has "magical breasts".

Hayek was recently in the headlines when she cured hunger in Sierra Leone, breastfeeding a local baby before allowing her breasts to be nationalized.

Speaking this morning at the launch of a new vaccine for democracy, a drug called WarVet45 that is administered via a lead pipe to the outside of the skull, Watmiwari said that the Zimbabwean government had long admired the people of Mexico.

He said that any nation that had found a way to employ 80 percent of its five-year-olds in the industrial sector was worth emulating.

"Plus they made Salma Hayek, and holy crap, is she well made," he added.

Watmiwari confirmed that Zimbabwe's President, Robert Mugabe, had been trying to get hold of Hayek to arrange an official viewing of her breasts, but that he had been unsuccessful so far.

"Comrade President Mugabe's phone is out of credit," said Watmiwari. "But he has sent her a 'please call me' and we are expecting a response very soon."

He added that actress Thandie Newton was being lined up as a possible backup plan.

"Thandie has Zimbabwean ancestry," he explained. "And she starred in something called 'Mission Impossible', which suggests she has all the right credentials for trying to save Zimbabwe."

Meanwhile the United Nations High Commission for Emergency Lactation has praised Zimbabwe's approach to the crisis.

"They're definitely on the right track with this idea," said spokesman Gilles Bustier-Corset.

"Ms Hayek seems to be a great solution. And if the breastfeeding thing doesn't work, we can always step in to organize mass screenings of her lap-dancing scene in 'From Dusk till Dawn'."

Hayek was not available for comment as she is currently in Afghanistan, negotiating a peace settlement between militant tribal elders and her breasts. ✪

CELEBRITY-HUNGRY AIRLINE PILOTS TO LAND PLANES IN RIVERS ACROSS GLOBE

Rescue services are bracing for a surge in emergency landings as celebrity-hungry airline pilots try to emulate Hudson River hero Chesley Sullenberger by ditching aircraft in rivers across the globe. Meanwhile Russian and former Soviet Bloc airline pilots have ridiculed the trend, saying that they have been landing Aeroflot aircraft in rivers for decades.

Captain Sullenberger has become an international celebrity since landing Flight 1549 on the Hudson River in January, and as airlines around the world continue to cut costs, demoralized pilots say their only option is to start emulating Sullenberger in the hope of scoring a lucrative book deal.

According to a spokeswoman from the International Air Transport Association, rescue services and air-traffic controllers are now preparing for a major uptick in river landings.

"It's a bit of an ultimatum," said spokeswoman Sabena Stuka. "The flying crews have made it clear that either we pay them more or they're going to try to belly-land on the 'New York Times' bestseller list by banging down on any trickle they see."

However, the threat has been dismissed by Russian and former Soviet bloc pilots, who say Western pilots are "girls".

Speaking to the media at the Aeroflot Academy of Excellence outside Minsk, where pilots are taught how to repair disintegrating airliners mid-flight using a Leatherman and a potato, veteran pilot Yevgeny Krashkors said river landings have been standard practice for the Russian carrier for decades.

"Rivers, canals, streams, millponds, sewage treatment plants, you name it," said Krashkors. "We've done it all.

"In fact we haven't landed an Aeroflot flight on a runway since 1983."

But not all national carriers have joined the move towards river landings.

This morning South African Airways confirmed that it had forbidden its pilots to ditch in any body of water in case consignments of drugs in the hold got soggy, while Air Zimbabwe has guaranteed passengers' safety, thanks to its policy of not taking off.

The policy was introduced in 2006 when the last of Zimbabwe's jet fuel was auctioned to pay for Grace Mugabe's hormone replacement therapy. Since then all inter-city flights in Zimbabwe have been towed by combine harvesters confiscated from counter-revolutionary farmers.

Air Congo said that while the Congo River offered plenty of scope for dramatic landings, the carrier would "probably not" attempt any landings on the river as it had run out of aircraft.

Air Congo spokesman Hercules Bamako said that the airline had landed its last Airbus on the Congo River in 2003.

"And when I say 'landed on', I really mean 'crashed into nose first'," he said.

"So no drama here. Just long hot summer days sitting behind a desk, watching the fan go round and round, and waiting for someone to sweep up the wreckage out on Runway Three."

OTHER BREAKING NEWS

★ **Co-worker drugged, put on plane, for relentless B.A. Baracus impression**

★ **Buckingham Palace denies plot to run over corgi in Paris tunnel**

★ **SABC to end all reports with "No, really, seriously."**

CHE PORTRAIT NAMED AS INTERNATIONAL SYMBOL OF ADOLESCENT POSEURS

NEW YORK. An elite panel of cultural advisors has unanimously selected the famous portrait of Argentinian revolutionary Ernesto 'Che' Guevara as the international symbol of adolescent poseurs. "Like the people who still celebrate the murderous little Marxist, it was a no-brainer," said one judge. "I mean, what do the last three letters of 'cliché' spell?"

Guevara rose to international prominence in the 1950s by growing facial hair at a time when most other South American warlords were clean-shaven, and by the early 1960s he had not only survived three attempted shavings at the hands of government troops but had managed to grow clandestine hairs in his nose, ears, and between his buttocks.

Speaking to a journalist at the award ceremony in New York last night where the portrait was named as the official symbol of adolescent poseurs, judge Carlos El Guapo said it was gratifying to see that Che was still touching lives after half a century.

"Fifty years ago he reached out, mostly through his extreme hotness, to the bored and stupid children of wealthy capitalists, and seduced them with his legend of sideburns at dusk, of goatees cutting through the Bolivian jungle.

"You wanted to follow Che to the ends of the earth, in case he'd sleep with you and impregnate you with his hairy little babies. I'm sure women felt the same.

"Today it's a little different, because obviously he's dead and so sleeping with him would be illegal in many countries. But he's still with us, convincing rich bored young white people with the hipness of Swiss yodellers that they're really edgy and engaged.

"It would be touching if it wasn't so incredibly pathetic."

Panelist Klaus von Papsmear added that Che's fashion sense had been key in establishing him as an icon of ignorant young poseurs.

"Che managed to make Marxism sexy," he said. "He really could have taught the Nazis quite a lot. Not least how to torture people using only rudimentary hair-care products. Che killed a lot of people, mostly without giving them a trial, but at least they looked hot when he dumped them in holes in the mud."

He said that Communism had killed far more people than the Nazis, but that the Nazis had made the fatal error of wearing lots of black leather that made them look extremely camp.

"Che was ahead of his time as a fashionista. He knew the only way he was going to be lauded for summarily executing whomever he wanted was to be adored by palpitating 20-year-old women in the US and Europe, and so he pioneered that whole jungle safari just-rolled-out-of-bed hotness.

"It was pure genius."

search results related to: cli ché

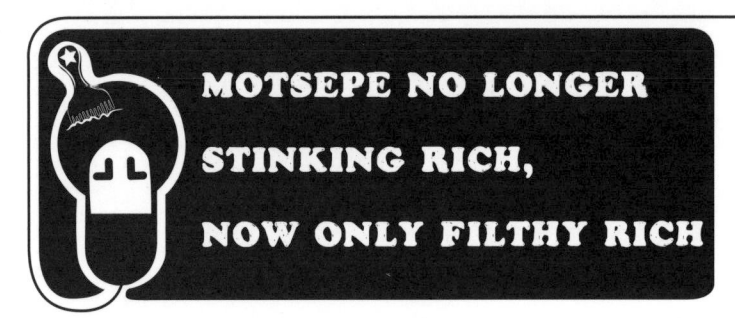

MOTSEPE NO LONGER STINKING RICH, NOW ONLY FILTHY RICH

JOHANNESBURG. The meltdown of the global economy has reportedly halved the fortune of South African tycoon Patrice Motsepe, leaving him only filthy rich.

According to the Forbes List of those most likely to be put up against a wall when the revolution comes, Motsepe had been stinking rich last year but will now have to cut back on lunches of nightingales' tongues.

This morning a stoic Motsepe confirmed that he had lost half his fortune in the past year, and was now worth only $1.3 billion. However, he said that he and his family were determined to find a way forward.

"At least we still have our health," he told journalists in the breakfast wing of his summer palace. "And faith that we can get through this."

The Forbes List, which appears annually and is used to gauge which of the world's elite will have their assets liquidated by firing squad should the poor ever discover how capitalism works, confirmed that Motsepe has slumped from stinking to filthy rich.

"It was a shock," conceded the tycoon. "Obviously I would have preferred to stay stinking rich.

"It's really hit me hard. As a man, as a husband, as a provider.

"I mean, no self-respecting man likes to stand in front of his family and tell them that family traditions are going to have to stop, like lighting the braai with Microsoft share certificates."

Asked how he and his family were going to cut back on expenses, Motsepe said that they had talked it through and decided to make certain sacrifices.

"For starters, no more nightingales' tongues on our lunch sandwiches," he said. "We can learn to like the lunchmeats that normal people eat, things like wild boar and snow leopard."

He also said that the family would have to start bathing in ass's milk instead of the imported condor albumen they had been using. "It'll be rough, but adversity breeds strength," said Motsepe.

Meanwhile the Forbes List has confirmed that the Oppenheimer family has managed to increase its net worth from $5 billion to $5.7 billion.

A spokesman for the family said they were delighted, but that they took nothing for granted and attributed their success to "lots of hard work, many wonderful friends, and a monopoly in a police state that supplied them with dirtcheap labour for 120 years."

SOMALI PIRATES STARTED REIGN OF TERROR WITH MIXED TAPES AT HOME

MOGADISHU. Many of the pirates operating off the coast of Somalia have admitted that they began their careers as international villains by recording music at home. "I first got a taste for piracy when I made a mixed tape for my girlfriend in 1992," said buccaneer Pugwash Mengistu. "When I saw the effect piracy had on women I just had to take it to the next level."

Speaking from the bridge of the captured Saudi tanker 'El Jibber Jabber', Mengistu said that the mixed tape had featured such hits as 'Eternal Flame' by the Bangles and 'Careless Whisper' by Wham.

"She just went off her face for it," he recalled.

"She thought it was the most romantic thing anyone had done since John Cusack stood with the boom-box over his head in 'Say Anything'."

He said subsequent girlfriends had reacted just as positively, and soon he was copying entire albums, before branching out into pirating DVDs.

Mengistu said his two biggest sellers at the Mogadishu Jolly Shopping Trolley supermarket had been 'Hai Hai Om Dai Ur Ta Wamu Neehai!', a Bollywood blockbuster about a singing assassin with magic hair who must dance his way into a fortified Pakistani harem to terminate the woman he adores, and 'Bridget Jones' Dowry'.

www.hayibo.com

"It is about a fat infidel who has the temerity to walk around showing her face and her legs," explained Mengistu. "However, she soon realises the error of her ways and seeks to marry so that she can produce sons."

According to US Navy piracy expert Rear-Admiral Black Dog "Chopper" Flint, Pugwash Mengistu's story is not unique.

"That's a pretty normal kind of progression for these guys," he explained.

"It usually starts with romantic ballads of the mid-80s, smiles and big hair, and ends with flamethrowers and money being dropped out of helicopters.

"Kind of like an episode of 'Knight Rider'."

He said that the anti-piracy push in the region was being hampered by the pirates' refusal to obey copyright laws.

"They've started producing cheap knock-offs of the same weaponry we're deploying against them," admitted Flint.

However, he said American sailors were learning to tell fake US warships from real ones.

"The knock-offs tend to have 'Hello Kitties' printed all over them, and the writing on the side says 'US of Amerika Navee Made In China'."

search results related to: aar aar

HOROSCOPE

Pisces Feb 19 - Mar 20

You're stuck in a rut this week, but look on the bright side. At least you're not stuck in a rut in Bloemfontein. Unless you are, in which case have you considered becoming addicted to morphine?

SHAIK SURVIVES FIRST NIGHT AT HOME, BUT TERMINAL CONDITION WORSENS

DURBAN. Convicted fraudster Schabir Shaik has reportedly survived his first night back in his luxury Durban mansion after serving 84 days of his 15-year prison sentence. Shaik's doctors have confirmed that he is in the final stages of a terminal condition called "life", and that the condition is irreversible. "We can only pray he makes it through the next 30 years," said one.

Shaik's medical parole ended the former businessman's harrowing prison ordeal, during which he spent 220 out of 304 days in a private hospital.

However, Shaik's personal physician and longtime friend, Dr Kildare Scott-Free, told journalists this morning that Shaik's prognosis was "very grim".

"Prisoners only get medical parole if they are in the final stages of a terminal condition," said Scott-Free.

"In Schabir's case, the ANC-approved parole board found that the condition in question was an awful and debilitating disease that we in the medical fraternity call 'life'."

He said that "life" had a zero-percent survival rate.

"Sufferers usually die within about 80 years of contracting the condition," he explained.

He confirmed that Shaik had survived his first night back at home, but that the condition had worsened slightly.

"Each day that goes past the sufferer loses about 24 hours," explained Scott-Free.

"Last night it was touch and go," he said. "At one point he couldn't find the remote for the plasma screen and his blood pressure shot up.

"But we managed to calm him down by showing him his latest bank statement."

Shaik recently received R5-million from the state as compensation for interest lost when his assets were seized following his convictions.

However, Scott-Free said that last night's emergency was a grim sign of things to come.

"We can't always be there to give him the remote and remind him how rich he is," he said.

"The outlook isn't good. I'm not sure Schabir will make it through the next 30 years.

"This really is the end."

Meanwhile the ANC has denied that it fast-tracked Shaik's parole because Jacob Zuma was running short of cash and needed "a little pick-me-up until payday."

www.hayibo.com

TAX SEASON BEGINS WITH PLAN TO FAST-TRACK CASH DIRECTLY TO CRIMINALS

PRETORIA. As tax filing season begins in earnest in South Africa, the SA Revenue Service has announced a groundbreaking initiative which will see it channeling funds directly from taxpayers to corrupt government officials and organized crime bosses. SARS said it would save billion of Rands that would otherwise have to be spent on "completely futile" law-enforcement.

SARS spokesman Lucretia Fisk said that it was time to cut out the middleman.

"It's very expensive being passive in the fight against crime," she said.

"South African taxpayers fork out enormous amounts of money every year to pay thousands of police, doctors, judges and coroners, and they're getting a pretty crap return on that investment.

"Nobody is naïve enough to believe that crime levels are anywhere close to dropping in the medium term, so it's time to be pragmatic and see what financial disciplines we can apply to a country with no functioning law-enforcement." She said the change in policy would be reflected on this year's SARS forms, which would allow taxpayers to choose which criminal element they would like their tax paid to.

She added that SARS offices were happy to deal with any queries.

"It can get quite complicated. Blue-collar versus white-collar crime, violent versus non-violent, work-related versus random hit-and-run, and so on. For example, a lot of people want to know if abductions count as deductions."

However not all allocations will be voluntary, and Fisk says that a compulsory Corruption Deduction will be included in next year's tax intake.

"South Africa loses around R50 billion a year to corrupt public officials.

"About 8 million people pay income tax, so we're looking at a deduction of R6,250 per taxpayer."

She explained that this amount would be automatically deducted from taxpayers and deposited directly into the personal savings accounts of senior municipal and local government officials. However, she added, taxpayers already stretched beyond their limits could either apply for an amnesty, or could consider becoming criminals themselves to benefit from the new cash infusion.

"Tax evasion is a well-established crime with a long and fairly proud tradition," said Fisk.

"If you choose not to pay the Corruption Deduction, or indeed any tax at all, we can register you as an Alternative Economic Resource Dependant, and whether you were Previously Disadvantaged or not we will assign you with official Currently Advantaged status, and you should get your first cheque about two months after filing." ★

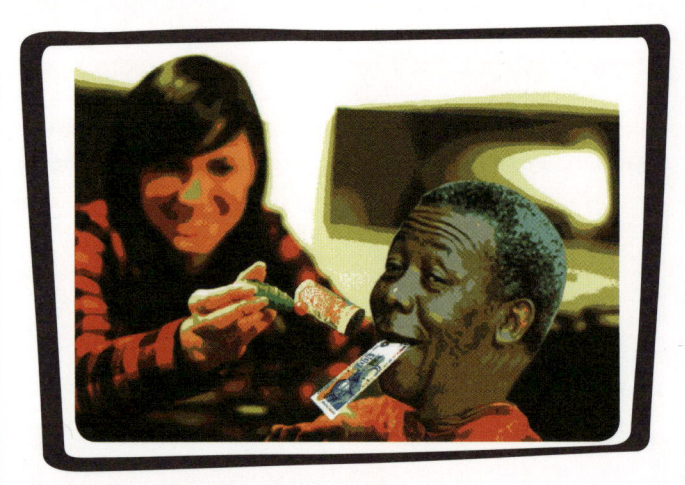

search results related to: channeling funds to corrupt government officials

SURVEY

The only way the opening ceremony of the 2008 Beijing Olympics could have been better was if:

○ Everybody was Kung-Fu fighting in the Heads of State area

○ Paris Hilton had been tricked into providing the climax to the fireworks display by being force-fed Sichuan food until she exploded

○ The hosts confirmed that Chinese is really just English spoken by a drunk and played backwards

○ The Chinese premier Hu Jintao admitted publicly that he is a sex-robot from the future

www.hayibo.com

ZUMA TO EMULATE OBAMA INAUGURATION EXCEPT BULLETPROOF GLASS TO BE IN FRONT OF CROWD

PRETORIA. Jacob Zuma has reportedly slammed his aides for planning a "totally kak" inauguration for him after seeing the pomp and ceremony of Barack Obama's historic swearing in as President. According to insiders, Zuma's ceremony was to have been based around traditional rituals such as a stripper jumping out of a cake.

The inauguration of Obama as the 44th President of the United States, the 14th Big Kahuna of Hawaii and the 2nd Grand Inquisitor of Guantanamo Bay, was watched by hundreds of millions of people around the globe, but Zuma insiders said his initial excitement quickly turned to rage when he saw the scale and sophistication of the event.

According to one witness, who wished to remain anonymous because he did not want to be metaphorically killed by Julius Malema, Zuma was "extremely distressed" by the short musical performance by a quartet of American greats that included cellist Yo-Yo Ma.

According to the witness, Zuma demanded to know if he was also going to get "a Chinese guy playing a massive violin" at his inauguration.

"We told him that Mr Ma was probably not available, but that we had found a girl in Brakpan who could play 'Awlethu' Mshini Wam 'on a saw, and a dog that could howl the first part of 'Nkosi Sikelel' iAfrika if you twisted its tail enough.

"He said those sounded 'awesome' but that he still wanted a Chinese guy with a massive violin, or else the whole day would be 'totally kak'."

Meanwhile the company that won the tender to organise Zuma's inauguration, Mthembu Chicken Farms and Industrial Solvents Inc, has conceded that it will have to rethink its original plans.

"We were pretty much going to focus the whole event around a stripper jumping out of a cake," said CEO Slasher Mthembu. "It seemed appropriate to Msholozi's whole political approach."

He said other plans that had been axed included a performance of 'I'd Do Anything for You; Dear' from the musical 'Oliver!' sung by Julius Malema; a praise poet telling an interesting parable about a crocodile and a steam-roller; and the symbolic hanging and burning of an effigy representing the South African judiciary.

However, he confirmed that one plan that would not change was the installation of a large barrier of bullet-proof glass.

"It's a lot like the one Barack had up in front of the podium," said Mthembu.

"Except it's about thirty times longer and it's going up in front of the crowd.

"It's not that we don't trust Mr Zuma, it's just that we don't want to cramp his style on his special day. If he wants to squeeze off a couple of slugs from his mshini while doing his victory dance up on the podium, far be it from us to rain on his parade."

search results related to: saw music

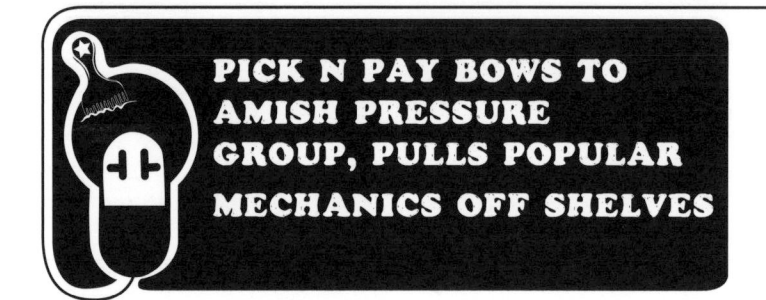

PICK N PAY BOWS TO AMISH PRESSURE GROUP, PULLS POPULAR MECHANICS OFF SHELVES

CAPE TOWN. Retail giant Pick 'n Pay has announced that it will withdraw the latest issue of 'Popular Mechanics' from its shelves following protests from Amish lobbyists who say that the magazine attacks their lifestyle and values. The move follows last month's decision by the retailer to pull student magazine 'Sax Appeal' from stores after complaints from offended Christians.

Attacks on Christianity and Jesus Christ unleashed a storm of protest against the University of Cape Town's student magazine in February, with many Christians abandoning meekness and a possible shot at inheriting the earth in favour of stinging attacks on the magazine's editorial team.

Pick 'n Pay subsequently pulled the issue from its shelves, agreeing that it was deeply insulting to Christian people.

Asked if it would pull gossip magazines 'You and Heat', both of which are deeply insulting to intelligent people, a spokeswoman for the retailer said that it "probably wouldn't".

"Religious beliefs are much more important than intelligent principles," explained Chastity Haliburton.

"Which is why we are taking the Amish protest very seriously. Even though they choose to live in the 16th century, and would rather die of gangrene than use an Elastoplast, it is a belief system and therefore beyond criticism."

According to Ms Haliburton a group of twelve Amish farmers staged their protest outside the Kommetjie branch of Pick 'n Pay yesterday morning, obstructing the entrance to the store with wooden wheelbarrows, a horse-drawn buggy, and five crates of women.

The protest lasted from 3am until 3.15am, at which point the farmers had to go home to make sure that their wives were not slacking over the butter churn.

According to the group's spokesman, Ezekiel Yoder, 'Popular Mechanics' was "the Devil working through the diabolical device of the printed word".

"This magazine openly mocks us and our way of life," said Yoder. "It strikes at the foundation of our beliefs."

Asked why the Amish had opted for protest instead of a traditional boycott of the store, Yoder admitted that they had in fact been boycotting Pick 'n Pay since it installed fridges and cash registers in the 1970s.

But he said their "hand had been forced" when they discovered the "satanic magazine" this week, after Esther Stoltzfus had been tempted into the store by the smell of freshly baked buns.

"She has been disciplined for her temptation," said Yoder, adding that she would be betrothed to Hideous Kurt Plank, the Seven-Fingered Boy, who had finished his community service last week.

SACP HAPPY TO RETAIN POWER WITHOUT CONTESTING ELECTION

PRETORIA. The South African Communist Party has turned down an invitation to run in the 2009 general elections, saying it is happy to continue dictating government policy without having to worry about petty details like having people actually vote for it. The party also reaffirmed its commitment to communism, saying it remained the only sure-fire way to get rich.

Speaking to journalists at the party's headquarters in the broom cupboard of the ANC's Luthuli House, SACP spokesman Trotsky Mtombela confirmed that the party had been invited to contest the elections but had decided to remain a "non-representative non-party not constrained by the apathy of the proletariat".

"People have said we should have the courage of our convictions and go it alone," said Mtombela, "but we wish to stress that so far we have no convictions, only allegations."

He added that the SACP was "perfectly content" dictating government policy without needing to test its popularity at the polls.

"The problem with voters is that they are much more difficult to lead around by the nose than senior ANC politicians," he explained.

"They ask difficult questions like, 'How can South Africa move towards communism when it depends entirely on the tax revenue from capitalists?' and 'When are you going to fix my shitty little RDP house?'

"That kind of question is just wildly unfair. ANC politicians don't ask questions like that. Instead they ask nice questions like, 'Would you like a piece of this tender action?' and 'Can I top up your drink there, Comrade?'"

He also rejected accusations that the SACP has enjoyed a parasitic relationship with the ANC.

"'Parasite' is such an ugly word," he said. "We like to think that our relationship with the ANC is much more like the love a young woodland creature shares with its powerful mother-figure.

"Which is why we will remain firmly attached to the teat of the mother sow, the African National Congress."

Meanwhile he said that the SACP leadership had recommitted itself to the ideology of communism during a weekend retreat at a luxury game lodge.

"You can say what you like, but South African communists continue to prove that communism is the only ideology that allows you to pull hefty monthly salaries, paid by the taxpayer, for doing pretty much nothing," said Mtombela.

"You don't have to woo voters, you don't have to listen to the complaints of your constituency, you don't even have to go to work, because nobody is totally sure what your job is.

"It's money for nothing and the chicks for free."

search results related to: mother sow

ESKOM VOWS TO KEEP LIGHTS ON, WILL BURN ZIM BANKNOTES

Embattled power distributor Eskom has won the praise of government after vowing to keep rolling blackouts to a minimum by burning Zimbabwean banknotes in some of its coal-fired power stations.

In a report to the Public Protector's office, handwritten by candlelight last week, Eskom committed itself to supplying the nation with electricity "equivalent to that supplied in major industrialised nations such as Bhutan and Chad."

According to the report, Eskom was "weeks away" from signing a deal with the Zimbabwean government that would see it stop burning coal and start burning wads of Zimbabwean currency.

Speaking to the media at the publication of the report, Eskom spokesman Sparkie Maloi said that the burning of banknotes solved numerous problems.

"The new Zimbabwean $10-million note is made of a compound of cow dung, Zam-Buk, and paraffin-infused blankets, and so it burns hotter and longer than coal," said Maloi. "Also, given the Zimbabwean exchange rate, it's currently cheaper to burn one kilogram of banknotes than one kilogram of coal."

He added that if the Harare Mint failed to keep up with supply, Eskom "might start burning the thousands of letters of complaint" the company received every day, but that this option was not sustainable since most letters were sent straight to the company's public relations office, which is currently housed in a dumpster on a nearby landfill.

However, Maloi was adamant that there was no crisis around energy supply.

"South Africans must understand that they currently enjoy a more plentiful and reliable supply of electricity than both the United States and Great Britain combined, in 1840. Both these countries are now world leaders."

The press conference was ended early when a blackout curtailed a PowerPoint presentation on how to heat a house using sunlight and a magnifying glass.

www.hayibo.com

OBAMA GIVEN NUCLEAR LAUNCH CODES, OPRAH'S PHONE NUMBER

WASHINGTON DC. With his inauguration just hours away, Barack Obama has reportedly been entrusted with the launch codes to the United States' nuclear arsenal and Oprah Winfrey's cell phone number. White House staff confirmed that once the new President was sworn in he would also be handed vouchers for dry-cleaning and takeout pizza, as well as a petrol card.

The launch codes and Winfrey's personal digits are considered the two most powerful sets of numbers in the world, and Washington insiders agree that they will present President Obama with unparalleled destructive capabilities.

However, Deputy Minister of Defense Shalom Tofu said that President Obama was eager to usher in a new era of diplomacy and tolerance, and would therefore probably favour Oprah over nuclear war in any showdown with the enemies of the United States.

"I think if it came to that, we'd see President Obama going Oprah instead of going nuclear," said Tofu.

"Given the choice between hundreds of thousands of deaths and hundreds of thousands of clichés, I think he'd be more comfortable dealing out the clichés."

He added that Obama was not avoiding conflict, but rather that he understood that most regimes were "actually just really sad inside" because they were fat or lonely or recently divorced, or were suffering from post-natal depression, or inadequate feminine hygiene.

"North Korea, Syria, Zimbabwe: these are places that really just want someone to listen to them and to give them a hug while they have a really good cry," said Tofu.

"That's a potential scenario for a tactical deployment of Oprah, yes, for sure."

White House secretary, Major Domo L'Uomo, also confirmed that Obama would be issued with presidential perks such as vouchers for dry-cleaning and takeout pizza, as well as a petrol card.

"Obviously there's more to being President than getting free stuff, but not a lot more," said L'Uomo, adding that Obama's vouchers would be redeemable anywhere within the Washington DC area, and were good for at least three months.

"If we weren't in a recession he'd probably also get a bottle of sparking grape juice on his pillow tonight and a bonbon for the wife, but the slowdown has hit all of us so they'll probably get a Coke and grape."

search results related to: calling oprah

OTHER BREAKING NEWS

★ **Gautrain revealed as slow botched robbery**

★ **SA to avoid recession by exporting narcotics on SAA**

www.hayibo.com

SAUDI ARABIA TO PUT HUMAN IN SPACE, WILL FIRST TEST ON WOMAN, CHIMP

RIYADH. Saudi Arabia says it intends to put a woman in space within five years and a human being within ten. According to a spokesman for the kingdom's newly formed space agency, tests are already underway in the Mysteries of Space-Sorcery laboratory in Riyadh. "Safety is our key concern," he said. "Hence we are testing on women, then dogs, and then chimps, in that order."

The spokesman, Prince Ali Ali Akhsenfri, also unveiled an artist's impression of the capsule that will take the first test subject, a woman called Leila, into space.

Shaped like a minaret and beautifully embossed with ancient Arabic designs and texts, the capsule also features a large viewing window which "may or may not have glass installed in it".

"If the subject's family wish us to install some glass, perhaps because they fear she will catch a cold from the breezes of deep space, then they are welcome to pay for it," said Akhsenfri.

He explained that the capsule was the result of years of development and represented a radical conceptual departure for engineers at the Mysteries of Space-Sorcery laboratory.

"Our first designs leaned fairly heavily towards flying carpets, Ottomans pulled by a team of wild geese, and white stags pursued by hounds that would leap off a cliff and into space," he said.

He said that these designs had wanted to reflect the lyricism and mystery of Arabian culture, while still getting the science right.

However, he said that early tests had been disappointing.

"The carpets tended to burn, or, if made in China, melt. Same thing with the geese, except obviously they didn't really ever melt, just sort of exploded as soon as we introduced the rocket fuel to the system.

"We also learned that white stags can only jump about ten or twenty feet in the air, and that they then develop considerable downward momentum."

But, he said, the new designs were a major step forward.

"We've opted for a minimalist interior: just a settee, a bowl of scented water, some maps of the cosmos, and a large lever. Forward to go, back to stop.

"We constantly had to keep in mind that we needed to make it simple enough for a woman to use."

He said once these basics had been got right, more complex technology would be introduced for tests piloted by dogs and chimps.

The press conference ended with a minute of silence in remembrance of former Space Vizier Abdul Hameed, who was crushed and killed in his laboratory by a falling white deer.

search results related to: woman in space

HOROSCOPE

Gemini May 21 - Jun 21

Worries at work will reach a climax as whispering behind your back turns to laughter, mime, and finally a float parade featuring burning effigies of you. Stay focused, and it will pass.

www.hayibo.com

SA EXPATS TOO BUSY EATING RATS TO VOTE

LONDON. South African expatriates living in Britain and the US say that they are unlikely to vote in April 22's general election as they are too busy queuing at soup kitchens and catching rats to bulk up their gruel. However, some expats have demanded the right to vote, hoping to stuff their shoes with ballot papers and gather up enough pencils to burn for warmth.

The issue of whether or not expatriates should be allowed to vote in the forthcoming election has been a political hot potato in South Africa, with the ANC opposing the move as it fears a strong expatriate turnout on April 22 could see its majority slip from 76 percent to 75.9 percent.

However, the Democratic Alliance and the Freedom Front Plus remain adamant that expatriates should be allowed to vote abroad, and are hoping for a major boost from this demographic.

4.4 million of South Africa's 4.5 million whites currently live in four flats in Shepherd's Bush in London, and both opposition parties are hoping to rouse at least a few dozen out of their traditional apathy come April 22.

But for expatriates, trapped in a crushing cycle of debt, joblessness and stale Jaffa cakes, voting is not as easy as it sounds.

Worsie van Tonder, a 26-year-old electrical engineer currently working as a coffee-bean titillator at Costa, says he is unlikely to vote even if allowed to.

"If you're out of the shop for more than twelve minutes a month they fire you," he explained. "I just don't know when I'd get the chance. And these beans need titillating."

Elsa-Chante Smit, 23, is a classically trained pet therapist but is currently paying her heating bills by working as an exotic dancer at Little Caesar's Skin Bar in Glasgow. She echoes Van Tonder's sentiments, although she says she's lucky just to have a job.

"A lot of South Africans in the UK, you see them roaming around in the streets like zombies. Slack jaws, moaning as they walk, Springbok jerseys all dirty and ragged, Springbok beanies all unravelling, Springbok scarves dragging in the slush behind them.

"The local kids throw them with rocks. Dogs rip off their jean-pants. It's horrible."

Brad Brad-Bradley, who decided to take a gap year in London with his friend and wrestling partner Chad Chadley-Chadford after they graduated from Michaelhouse with distinctions in suppressed masculine rage, said he would not be voting on April 22 as he would be at the South African embassy applying for economic refugee status.

"Bru, we're so stoked about going home and that, but we sold our Bok puffer jackets and Bok jerseys so we'd totally freeze to death before we made it to Heathrow," he explained.

He said getting on a South African Airways flight was easy as one only needed to offer the cabin crew some hard drugs.

"The problem is that me and Chad ate our drugs last night, with the last of the rat.

"It was so cold, and our teeth are starting to get loose in our gums, and he had this brick of skunk, so we fried it in diesel oil and shredded the last of the rat-leg into it.

"It tasted lank kak but what can you do in these times?"

search results related to: expat rat

MORE LIES AS CARL NIEHAUS ADMITS HE IS DIVORCED MOTHER OF FOUR

PRETORIA. Disgraced former ANC spokesman Carl Niehaus admitted to yet more lies this morning, just hours after media claims that some of his qualifications had been faked. Speaking to journalists from inside the cardboard box he now calls home, Niehaus confessed that he is in fact Hestrie van Tonder, a 52-year-old divorced mother of four from Boksburg.

Niehaus' revelations have dominated national headlines this week, as first his financial dealings and then his tertiary qualifications were exposed.

The ANC has reportedly put pressure on Niehaus to provide full disclosure after the party became unsettled by claims he was making around the office that he had once wrestled a grizzly bear to death while making love to identical Swedish sextuplets.

"It sounded unlikely," said ANC spokesman Cremora Khumalo. "Four Swedish twins and a koala bear, perhaps. Maybe three and some sort of wolverine or badger if he'd warmed up properly beforehand. But not all six plus the grizzly."

He said the claims had been discussed at Cabinet level and the party had felt that with Julius Malema in government there was only room for one senior party member to be making "completely insane assertions", and so Niehaus was asked to disclose everything.

According to Khumalo, Niehaus had torn off his clothes, revealing a slightly stained petticoat and brassière, and had rushed from the room in tears.

Journalists tracked down Niehaus this morning sitting in a cardboard box outside the mansion he is being evicted from. It was there that he confessed to being Hestrie van Tonder, a 52-year-old divorced mother of four from Boksburg.

"I just wanted to do right by my kids," she sobbed. "At first it was just little white lies so I could pay the rent. I told people I had a diploma from a typing college, stuff like that."

But she said the lies quickly spiralled out of control.

"Soon I would go to an interview for a temporary secretarial post and they'd ask me if I could work a switchboard, and I'd say yes, because I had been the South African ambassador to the Netherlands, and they'd say 'Sjoe!' and I'd get the job."

Asked why she had claimed to have a Doctorate in Theology from the University of Utrecht, Van Tonder said she had once accidentally blasphemed during an interview.

"I was applying for a job at Crazy Solly's Pink Bubble Laundry there by the dog track, and I touched a hot iron and I took the Lord's name in vain.

"Crazy Solly said he didn't like blasphemy, and I said, 'No, it's okay because I'm a professional, I've got a Doctorate in Theology from Utrecht', and Crazy Solly said, 'Shit a brick!' and gave me the job.

"It just sort of stuck."

Asked how she had gone from working in a laundry to being a senior figure in the ANC, she explained that doing dry-cleaning and being an ANC spokesman were "basically the same job".

"They bring you dirty laundry, you make the dirt go away, and they pay you in cash," she said.

"You never ask questions, you never make eye contact. Just work the machine, take the money, and do right by your kids."

search results related to: tell me lies

www.hayibo.com

ANC ELECTION MANIFESTO IS TIME WARP FROM 'ROCKY HORROR PICTURE SHOW'

PRETORIA. The ANC had denied that its recently revealed election manifesto is a badly plagiarized version of 'The Time Warp' from 'The Rocky Horror Picture Show'. However, it has acknowledged that its new policy is "just a jump to the left, and then a step to the right", and calls on cadres to put their hands on their hips and bring their knees in tight.

Political commentators had been eagerly awaiting the unveiling of the new manifesto amid growing speculation over whether the ANC would promise its voters unbridled bliss or the granting of three wishes.

However, many pundits say they were extremely unsettled by the unveiling of the manifesto last week as it seemed to have been lifted intact from 'The Rocky Horror Picture Show'.

The unveiling took place at the Queen Amidala of Naboo Stadium in the Eastern Cape, where ANC President Jacob Zuma told thousands of supported that it was astounding how time was fleeting and how madness had taken its toll.

He asked voters to listen closely, not for very much longer, adding that he was determined to keep control.

He also warned the ANC faithful to be on its guard against subversive forces.

"I was walking down the street just having a think when a snake of a guy gave me an evil wink," said Zuma.

He said it had shaken him up and taken him by surprise, and added that the man had had "a pick-up truck and devil's eyes".

He would neither confirm nor deny that he was referring to the leadership of COPE.

However, observers said they became suspicious when Zuma urged the audience to take a jump to the left and then a step to the right in 2009, after which they should put their hands on their hips and bring their knees in tight.

"But it was the pelvic thrust that really drove them insane," said one observer who wished to remain anonymous.

"And that's when we realised he was doing the 'Time Warp' again."

Meanwhile the ANC has strongly denied any plagiarism, but has promised to follow up on the similarities between its policy document and 'The Rocky Horror Picture Show' to make sure there has been "no mischief caused by recently deposed sweet transvestites from transsexual Transkei".

search results related to: transsexual transkei

SURVEY

Obama's battle cry was "Yes We Can!" Which of our parties' slogans would win you over in 2009?

○ ID: "Yes We. You LIE! You LIE!"

○ ANC: "No We Didn't! Who Told You? No I wasn't! Where's Your Proof?"

○ DA: "No We Can't But We'll Make Jolly Sure They Can't Either!"

○ UDM: "Yes I Can Because I'm Bantu Holomisa, Who Are You?"

○ ACDP: "No You Can't Because the Old Testament Forbids It!"

SOVEREIGN SA BANS DALAI LAMA, WILL CALL CHINESE PREMIER "BAAS"

PRETORIA. The South African government has defended its decision to ban Tibet's Dalai Lama from entering the country and has denied that it is slavishly obeying China. According to a spokesman, the government has made only minor concessions to Beijing, such as promising to give the Chinese Premier erotic massages on demand and calling him "baas".

The decision to ban the exiled Tibetan leader follows days of speculation over how low the government would bend over to please China, with many experts predicting a full kowtow on all fours.

However, according to insiders there is still some confusion within government, as dozens of Ministers and Deputy Ministers did not know who the Dalai Lama was and thought media personality Dali Tambo was being refused entry to South Africa.

"I have known Dali Tambo for years and I had no idea he was a Tibetan terrorist monk," said ANC backbencher Blimpy Mokoena.

"It just goes to show you never really know people."

According to government spokesman Tjoepstil Shabangu the state had also briefly considered banning Dali Tambo but decided that the Dalai Lama was more dangerous.

He went on to defend South Africa's sovereign status, saying that the country acted completely independently of China except when it didn't.

"We reject with contempt the allegation that we are a puppet of Beijing," said Shabangu.

"A client, maybe, depending on what terms they force us to take. A vassal, definitely. But not a puppet. Never a puppet."

He said that recent talks between Pretoria and Beijng had reaffirmed the mutual respect the two countries had for each other.

"They reaffirmed how much they respect our raw materials, and we reaffirmed how much we respect their money," he said.

He acknowledged that South Africa had been forced to make some concessions to China in order to keep Chinese exports flowing, but that these had been "minor".

"So what if we have to call them 'baas' and give their Premier an erotic massage whenever he's in town?

"It's a small price to pay for access to wonderful Chinese exports like inflatable dolphins and busloads of rude tourists."

President Kgalema Motlanthe could not be reached for comment as he was reportedly serving as a porter and gun-bearer for a party of Chinese industrialists shooting endangered wildlife in Limpopo.

search results related to: dalai and dali

www.hayibo.com

ORANIA LEADERS LAUD MALEMA'S FINE MIND, HEALTHY ATTITUDE TO WOMEN AND RACE

ORANIA. The leaders of the whites-only enclave of Orania in the Northern Cape have lauded ANC Youth League president Julius Malema for his clear thinking on race and gender issues, saying that they and Malema have much in common, including a love of the South African soil, a passionate devotion to the well-being of their people, and an IQ of roughly 55.

Malema's aides say he had not intended to visit Orania on the weekend, but had arrived there by accident after trying to instruct his GPS navigation system to take him to the Oranje Minimart in Hillbrow where he wanted to buy a packet of Nik Naks.

According to friend and bodyguard Stalin Romotswe, Malema began to suspect that he had made an error after about five hours, when he saw the skeleton of a camel protruding from a sand dune.

However, Malema had refused to turn back, saying that ANC pioneers never admitted an error, even if it meant wasting huge amounts of time and money.

Malema's arrival in Orania reportedly caused a sensation, as many residents had not previously known that black people were allowed to drive cars.

However, once traditional gifts such as copper beads and animal pelts had been exchanged, residents said they found Malema to be a "deep thinker on important issues".

"We see eye to eye on so many things," said Orania spokesman Abraham Bittereinder.

"For example his views on gender are very refreshing, and suggest that government isn't just rolling over to the insane demands of the barren and man-hating career women and their homosexual toadies."

He also said that Malema's views on race were virtually identical to those of Orania, with a strong emphasis on the importance of race in everyday life.

"Mr Malema also represents an increasingly insular African tribe," he said. "Both our tribes see persecution everywhere, and we both base our nationalist claims on the Bible and a concept called 'freedom' which is never accurately defined so that we can manipulate it as we see fit."

He added that he "probably shouldn't have said that last bit", but said that making "stupidly revealing comments" was another trait shared by both Malema and the Orania community.

Meanwhile Malema was reportedly impressed by the residents' woodworking skills.

With a small economy and limited access to raw materials, Orania relies heavily on traditional woodworking, and along with wooden furniture and wooden transportation such as donkey-drawn wheelbarrows, many townsfolk sport wooden legs, wooden dentures and wooden heads.

UFS URGES NEW BLACK RECTOR TO KEEP TRIBAL RHYTHMS AND STABBING-SPEARS TO HIMSELF

BLOEMFONTEIN. The announcement that the University of the Free State has appointed a black man as rector has been met with alarm by students who have warned Professor Jonathan Jansen not to make drastic changes at the institution widely regarded as the country's 57th best high school. They have also urged Jansen not to make any sudden moves, or eye contact.

The University made national headlines in 2008 when a racism scandal rocked the country and caused the closure of the Reitz Hostel and forced the History Department to admit to students that it was no longer 1963.

This morning a spokesman for UFS said that education expert Jansen would be welcomed "for at least 48 hours".

"Obviously after that he needs to report to a police station to extend his permit to stay in the Free State," explained Dr Worsie Mosbol.

He also urged Jansen not to make any sudden moves, or to "get fresh with white women", even if he was a Fulbright Scholar.

"Professor Jansen must remember that this is the University of the Free State. We're not impressed by academic qualifications," he said.

www.hayibo.com

He added that his cousin Puisie Nel had been awarded a Halfbright Scholarship to the Christian Vengeance Wrestling Academy in Ficksburg, which proved that "scholarships mean fokkol".

He acknowledged that many at UFS were anxious about the changes Jansen was planning to make at an institution that has regularly been named as one of the top 100 high schools in the country.

"Yes, people are nervous," said Mosbol. "If you've studied anthropology or history at UFS, as I have, you know what black people are like, with all the stabbing-spears and the drums and the polygamy and that."

But, he said, as long as Jansen kept his "tribal rhythms" relatively quiet after 10pm and refrained from wearing bones in his nose during board meetings, most UFS staff would soon learn to tolerate him.

Most important of all, he said, Jansen's appointment would help UFS mirror the broader South African experience.

"There's a non-elected black official running everything, a small group of wealthy white people who pay his salary, and then a large mass of poor black people that both the leader and the white people ignore."

He said the racism row had come as a profound shock to many students at UFS, who had not realized that black people had feelings that could be hurt. However, he said, a period of soul-searching had resulted in an overhaul of labour policy.

"We are definitely reforming," he said. "Before, we mainly employed blacks for throwing clay pigeons for the shooting club, but now we let them hold the tackle bags at rugby."

search results related to: black tackle bag

RECESSION FORCES AMY WINEHOUSE TO MINE NOSE FOR UNDISCOVERED COCAINE

LONDON. Troubled pop diva Amy Winehouse says the global financial crisis will force her to mine pockets of cocaine still lying undisturbed in her nose. According to a statement by the singer, carved on a bathroom stall in Soho, narcotic geologists predict that there might still be up to fifteen grams of cocaine lodged in her nose ready for extraction.

The global credit crunch has seen narcotics prices surge as a wave of unemployed derivatives traders upgraded social drug-taking habits into full-time dependencies.

The closure of South African Airways' state-sponsored drugs trafficking service has also squeezed supply dramatically, and the airline is also refusing to answer questions about when it plans to re-open its supply routes, saying that strategic planning will have to wait until it has managed to fence a consignment of heroin to an East Asian buyer to pay departing CEO Khaya Ngqula's severance package.

Many experts believed that Winehouse's nose had been fully exploited and that soaring cocaine prices would see her having to resort to snorting lines of coffee creamer, reportedly a poor substitute for mood-altering drugs.

However, after a groundbreaking survey of her nasal passages, narcotic geologists say there is strong evidence of residual cocaine.

Speaking to the media this morning, legendary drug prospector Charlie Snow said that he had glimpsed stalactites and stalagmites near Winehouse's sinuses that could be compressed cocaine.

"Obviously we don't want to put the cart before the horse, or the crack before the whore, as it were, but at this time it looks promising," said Snow.

He said further tests would be done to determine whether the formations were made from cocaine or were simply the left-overs of a kebab Winehouse reportedly used as a pillow outside a club last week.

"If it's genuine blow we'll be going in later this month," he explained. "It's called a rhinoblasty. Basically it's strip-mining with very mild medical explosives on a very small scale.

"There will be some bruising, but nothing that half an inch of base and mascara can't fix."

According to the statement from the singer, carved with a nail file into the door of a toilet stall, Winehouse is "excited and excited, plus excited".

She explained that it was "quite a big nose and things get lost in it all the time", including fast food and small pets, but she said that she had never been expecting the bonus of free drugs.

"This is a wonderful way to start 2024," she wrote.

www.hayibo.com

SCUFFLE IN OVAL OFFICE AS ZUMA ASKS FOR MACHINE GUN

WASHINGTON DC. U.S. authorities have confirmed that a "brief scuffle" took place in the Oval Office of the White House yesterday morning after South African leader Jacob Zuma asked to be handed his machine gun during a meeting with President George W. Bush. Secretary of State Condoleezza Rice is reportedly "flustered but fine" after being used as a human shield.

Zuma, the president of the ruling African National Congress, is currently on a visit to the United States where he is trying to reassure foreign investors that they will not be put in a pot, boiled and eaten if they come to South Africa.

According to White House spokesman Ecclesiastes Norris, the scuffle allegedly broke out while Zuma and Bush were exchanging traditional greetings.

"President Bush had just finished demonstrating how to rope a steer and was removing the lasso from around Secretary Rice's shin, when Mr Zuma broke into song," said Norris.

He confirmed that the song had been Zuma's war-cry, 'Awlethu' Mshini Wam'.

He said Bush had been captivated and had complimented Zuma on the "crazy Afro jive and pumping tribal rhythms".

The President had then asked what "Awlethu' mshini wam" meant.

When told it translated as "Bring me my machine gun", Bush reportedly stopped kneeling on Rice's neck and hauled her up in front of him as a human shield.

Norris said that Bush's Secret Service minders had finally persuaded him to release the Secretary of State by briefly rendering him unconscious with a Vulcan sleeper grip to the neck.

However, he said, Bush remained indignant after coming to, telling Zuma that "going all jungle fever might wash with Obama but there's still a white man in this office, you dig?"

Once order had been restored, the two leaders discussed the international financial crisis, at which point Bush reportedly offered to buy South Africa with the money in his wallet. He apologized for not being able to pay more for the country but explained he had spent $10 on a pizza the night before and hadn't been to an ATM yet.

However, Zuma declined, saying that cash transactions "always ended in tears with shredded faxes and unpleasant and hurtful recriminations".

The meeting ended cordially with an exchange of official gifts, said Norris. He confirmed that Bush had given Zuma some beaver pelts, copper beads and a musket with the firing pin removed, while Zuma gave the American President a pass for the 2006/07 season at uShaka Marine World in Durban.

search results related to: bring me my machine gun

www.hayibo.com